GODDESSES
HEROES AND
SHAMANS

THE YOUNG PEOPLE'S GUIDE TO
WORLD MYTHOLOGY

GODDESSES
HEROES AND
SHAMANS

THE YOUNG PEOPLE'S GUIDE TO
WORLD MYTHOLOGY

SCHOLASTIC INC.

New York Toronto London Auckland Sydney
Mexico City New Delhi Hong Kong

ISBN 0-439-15385-9

12 11 10 9 8 7 6 5 4 3 2 1   9/9 0 1 2 3 4/0

Printed in the U.S.A.   14

First Scholastic printing, November 1999

Edited by Cynthia O'Neill, Peter Casterton, Catherine Headlam
Designed by Ch'en Ling, Terry Woodley, Karin Ambrose, John Jamieson
Art edited by Christina Fraser

Contributors:
What is a Myth?, Mediterranean Lands: David Bellingham
Northern Lands: Dr. David M. Jones
Africa: Margret Carey
Eastern Asia: Louise Tythacott
Central and South America, South Pacific Lands: Kathleen McPhilemy

The publishers would like to thank Adrian Cunningham,
Department of Religious Studies, Lancaster University, England,
for his assistance in preparing this book.

·CONTENTS·

· ABOUT THIS BOOK ·

Goddesses, Heroes, and Shamans contains over 500 characters from myths around the world. Some are well-known; others may be new to you.

A myth is more than just a good story, as *What is a Myth?* explains. The patterns and themes that appear in mythologies around the world are introduced here.

Short essays introduce the different peoples and their mythologies. They are followed by A to Z sections that list major mythic characters. Where another character's name appears in SMALL CAPS, it means that more information about them can be found in a different entry. The colorful, imaginative illustrations will help to bring the myths to life again.

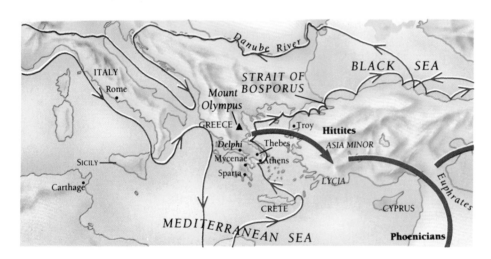

You can look up the meanings of some unusual words on page 154—such as avatar, oracle or shaman. Finally, on page 155 there is an index listing every character.

Each geographical section opens with a map, showing the people and places mentioned in the text. Knowing where important cities and areas were in relation to each other will help you to understand how myths spread and why so many stories are similar in different areas. A time line gives important dates, so that you can see when a civilization flourished.

▶ *Boxes provide extra information on people's customs and beliefs. Look for facts about sources, forms of worship, or other useful details.*

To ensure good harvests and victory in battle, the Vikings made sacrifices to the gods at major festivals: Vetrarblot, held in October, Jolablot in January and Sigrblot in April. There was much feasting and drinking during the festivals.

· WHAT IS A MYTH? ·

The word "myth" comes from an ancient Greek word, "mythos," which means "a spoken or written story." People often think of a myth as simply a story, but this is not the complete picture. A myth is a story with a purpose. Generally, it tries to explain the way the world is or the relationship between gods and goddesses, and human beings. Although the events that take place may seem impossible, the message behind the story may have an important religious or social meaning. The message sets myths apart from ordinary stories.

People have always tried to understand the world's mysteries. They have looked for answers to questions as varied as "Who made the universe?" to "What causes a storm?" to "Why are humans different from animals?"

Atotaroh, page 24

Myths were developed so people could make sense of the different things that happened to them. This is why every society has had its own collection of myths—known as its mythology.

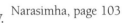
Narasimha, page 103

Why do myths survive?
Some myths have survived for thousands of years. One reason for this is that in most societies myths play an important role in religion. They confirm people's beliefs and preserve them for future generations. Such stories are recorded in pictures, written down, or passed on by word of mouth.

Of course, a myth is also much more likely to survive if it tells a good story. Many myths are told to teach people how to behave properly. To get their message across, they need to hold their audience spellbound right from the start.

Good against evil

Myths are often concerned with right and wrong. What is thought of as good and what is evil differs from one society to another, but most mythologies include beings who bring pain and trouble to people, as well as those who protect and comfort them. An evil monster will be defeated by bravery, strength, and cunning, but the hero's and villain's actions are also intended to show people the benefits of choosing between good and bad behavior. In return for good behavior the hero is rewarded with a prize—often eternal life—while the villain receives some terrible punishment, showing that evil does not pay.

The Archer Yi, pages 110, 115

Gods and goddesses

Another important role of mythology is to explain the relationship between human beings and divine beings. The nature of gods and goddesses changes from one mythology to another; however, deities tend to reflect the ideals of the people who worship them and are exceptionally quick-witted, or beautiful, or strong, and so on. The ruling Inca family claimed to be descended from a god; this made their authority stronger.

Quite a few societies believe in a powerful, aloof, supreme god who is surrounded by many minor gods and spirits. Some peoples see the gods as human in form and behavior: the Greek divinities often act like ordinary humans and can be jealous or spiteful. Other societies see the divine powers as the spirits behind the elements of nature, such as the Sun.

Gods and goddesses are not always thought of as looking like, or even being, human. For example, in myths from North America and Siberia, animals and birds have the status of gods. In Egyptian and Near Eastern mythology, the gods are a mixture of human and animal forms, such as the jackal-headed Egyptian god ANUBIS. Although gods or goddesses might sometimes visit human beings, they are believed to live outside the world. Very often their home is in a land found above the Earth (Heaven) or below it (called the Underworld). Heaven, Earth, and the Underworld are sometimes linked by a World Post or World Tree: examples are found in Norse and Siberian mythology.

Creation myths

Yanauluha, page 30

Many myths describe the creation of the universe, or the origin of the natural world and of human beings. This is often the act of a creator god or goddess who exists before anything else, such as PTAH, the Egyptian god, or the Finnish goddess, ILMATER. Although the divinities involved in the creation vary from myth to myth, the basic stories are often the same.

Creation myths usually begin with nothingness: the universe has no shape or form. Out of this "nothing" the natural elements such as the Sun, the Moon, or the Earth appear one by one. These are often named as gods and goddesses. Some African and Asian myths describe how winds stirred up water and soil into a whirling mixture, which finally settled to become the heavy Earth with the sky above. The sky then watered the Earth, and life appeared.

A similar Greek myth exists in which the Earth and sky appear from chaos, but here the Earth and sky become the female GAIA and the male URANUS.

Indian, Egyptian, and Japanese myths see these first elements as joined together in a huge egg, floating in space. All life is then born from the egg.

The first humans

In some mythologies, the first humans are descended from a half animal, half human ancestor. In some Native American myths they are led onto Earth's surface from underground. In other myths, people grow like plants. In a myth from China, NU WA creates the first human beings just because she is lonely.

In many mythologies people soon offend the gods and are punished by a devastating flood that practically destroys the human race. This occurs in North American, Indian, Near Eastern, Greek, and Southeast Asian myths. One family may survive to begin the human race again. (*See* MANU and UTANAPISHTIM.)

Nu Wa, pages 114, 115

Heroic humans

Every mythology has its heroes—humans who perform extraordinary feats of bravery or go on fantastic journeys. They vary from one culture to another, depending on the ideals of each society. All heroes seem to have certain features in common, however.

The hero tends to be a man, mainly because most civilizations were ruled by men. Women who do behave heroically tend to be acting alongside men, though there are exceptions. However, in Greek mythology heroes are helped and watched over by the goddess ATHENA.

Valkyrie, page 53

Sometimes the hero has one mortal and one divine parent, such as OLOFAT, the Micronesian hero who was the son of the Sun god. They may have immense physical strength; often their intelligence is tested too. The hero pursues a quest, frequently to find a sacred object. Along the way he saves people from monsters and may be badly wounded, only to be healed by magic. At the end of his quest, the hero may be rewarded by becoming a god himself.

Culture heroes

A "culture hero" is a character who acts with skill, daring, or cunning to establish the basis of human society. For example, such a hero may bring fire to his people or teach them the rules of civilized society. These characters are normally, but not always, male. In the mythology of the Lakota from North America, a woman first brought the people their sacred pipe (see page 23).

The afterlife

Many myths exist to explain what happens after death. There are often a number of different places where people go when they die, depending on their actions in this world. In Norse mythology, for example, warriors who die bravely in battle are carried through the sky by VALKYRIE maidens to a hall called VALHALLA.

Wicked people are punished in the afterlife, spending eternity in various Hells or Underworlds, in which they are dreadfully tormented by demons.

Animals

Animals play an important role in all mythologies. Not surprisingly, they are a more common feature of farming or hunting cultures. In Siberian culture, people hunted the brown bear but at the same time gave it powers like those of the gods. In South American mythology, the jaguar is granted great respect and many stories surround it, including myths that explain why its flesh must not be eaten.

Semidivine animals, such as the winged horse PEGASUS, play an important role in Greek mythology. In Africa, creatures such as HARE (*see below*) and Spider frequently appear in the myths. In China the heroic adventures of MONKEY are well-known.

Trees and natural springs are often believed to contain spirits, which become angry if the tree is damaged or the water source is polluted. These nature myths show early human interest in protecting the environment by granting such objects

Loki and Idunn, page 49

magical powers. In Scandinavian mythology there is even a World Tree, whose health reflects the state of the environment.

Fabulous beasts

All mythologies have their own supernatural beasts, just as today we have space monsters who appear in science fiction films. These fantastic monsters are worthy enemies for the heroes who conquer them and become saviors of the people. The most common form of monster is a serpent. These appear in different forms, from the many-headed monstrous Hydra defeated by the Greek hero HERACLES, to the dragons found in Asian and Celtic myths.

Sacred places

In every culture, certain places are seen as holy or sacred because they are the site of some mythical event. When people live in close harmony with nature—as with the Australian aboriginals, Native American, or African cultures—they may consider pools, mountains, caves, and other features of the landscape to be sacred places. They may leave objects and paintings to local spirits in these places: for example, cave paintings are important in aboriginal belief.

A "soul catcher," used by a North American shaman to cure a sick person.

These sacred places may be visited during a journey made by young people as part of their acceptance into adult society. There are also ritual festivals at certain sites: for example, totem poles mark a sacred spot and are the center of dance rituals.

More urban cultures built temples on sacred spots where they believed deities lived while on Earth. Many of these buildings stayed in the country even when people had moved into the cities. Every temple held festival days to honor the gods.

Contacting the gods

Humans communicate with the gods and goddesses in various ways. In some mythologies, the divine beings are called upon for help with hymns, prayers, and sacrifices. In every society, male or female priest figures were believed to provide a contact between the world of myth and the present world. These figures also taught myths to their people.

The gods or spirits can also be reached by means of a shaman (a man or woman who is able to contact or communicate with the spirit world). Shamans have existed in many cultures. They use myths to guide people in and out of the spiritual world. The power of myth is shown in the respect paid to these figures by their societies.

Temple of Amen-Ra, page 74

Where did myths come from?

For centuries, people have wondered where myths first came from. Over 2,000 years ago, a Greek scholar called Euhemerus suggested that all myths are based on historical events and that the original facts have become exaggerated as time passed. More recently, scholars have developed other theories, including the suggestion that all myths were originally symbolic stories (which means that the people and events in them represent ideas). However, there is no one theory with which everybody agrees.

Why is mythology important?

Studying the mythology of a people helps us to understand them. The myths of a past civilization, combined with the historical evidence and the discoveries made by archaeologists, can give us clues to how that society thought and what the lives of the people were like.

When we read the myths that a people tell, we learn more about their customs and values and can compare them to our own. For example, many myths about the sea are found in the South Pacific. This reflects the people's sea-going way of life. Myths from ancient Egypt show that people were concerned about death and the afterlife.

Mythologies around the world may have different details but have surprisingly similar themes in common.

Pahmuri-Mahse, page 137

People everywhere seem to have asked the same kind of questions about the universe and have shared the same hopes and fears.

One definition of myth, as simply a traditional religious story, would include features of the Jewish, Christian, and Muslim religions. Not everybody agrees with this definition. It is not used in this book, although elements of Jewish and Arabic folklore, as well as some of the legends of the Christian saints, are similar to myths that are contained here.

· NORTHERN · LANDS

The peoples of Siberia and the Inuit of the Arctic and sub-Arctic are descendants of people who migrated from central Asia thousands of years ago. The ancestors of the Inuit and Native Americans crossed into America during the last ice age. At that time the sea level was lower and there was dry land where the Bering Strait is today. Myths from Siberia and the Arctic originally stem from the beliefs of people who lived in Asia during the last ice age. To a lesser extent, this is true of Native American mythologies as well.

In northern Europe, the cultures of the Celtic, Slavic, and Norse peoples emerged gradually between 600 B.C. and A.D. 400. European myths contain some elements that seem to derive from the ancient Near East and even India. But the details of each mythology developed locally.

Although they have roots in different places, these mythologies have broad themes in common. Most societies believed in a supreme god of some kind, but thought that other, lesser gods controlled the forces of nature. In each community, certain individuals were believed to have extrapowerful links with the spirits. Each culture had its own creation myth, and many believed in a complex universe, made up of several different worlds, linked by a World Tree or World Post.

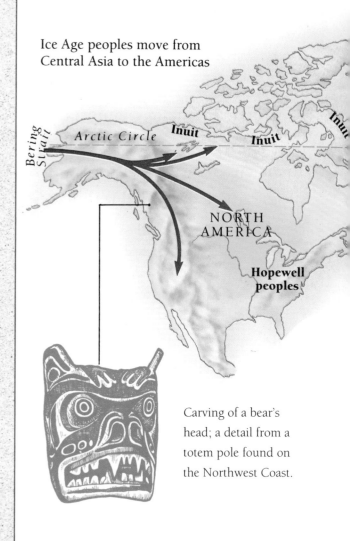

Ice Age peoples move from Central Asia to the Americas

Carving of a bear's head; a detail from a totem pole found on the Northwest Coast.

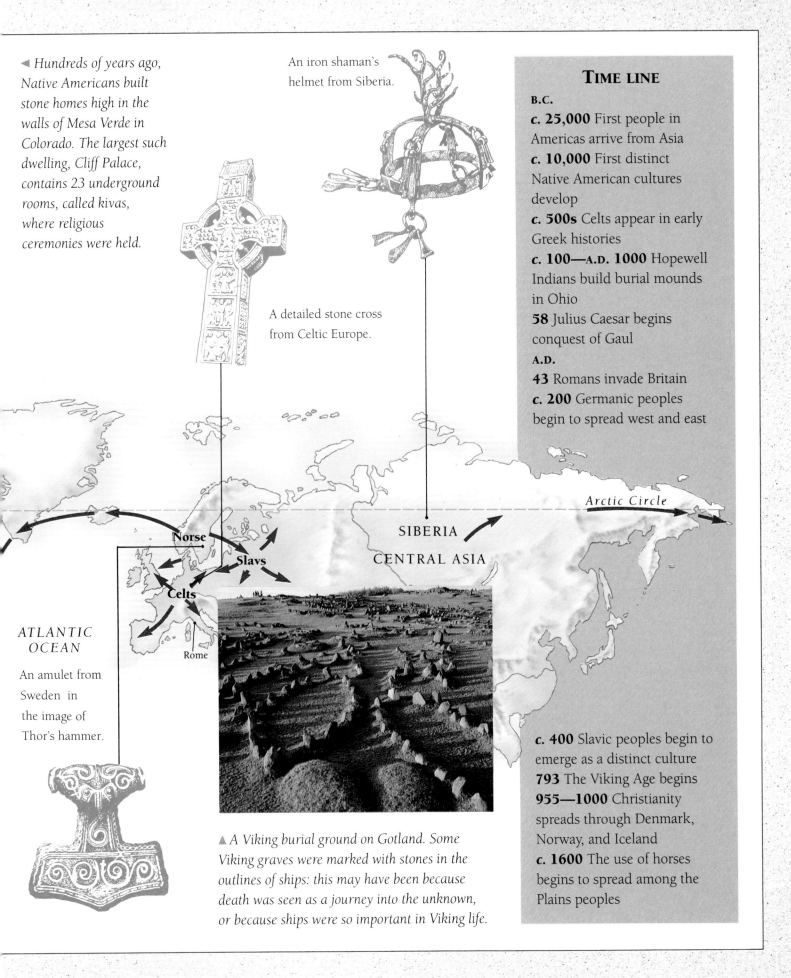

◀ Hundreds of years ago, Native Americans built stone homes high in the walls of Mesa Verde in Colorado. The largest such dwelling, Cliff Palace, contains 23 underground rooms, called kivas, where religious ceremonies were held.

An iron shaman's helmet from Siberia.

A detailed stone cross from Celtic Europe.

ATLANTIC OCEAN

An amulet from Sweden in the image of Thor's hammer.

Norse

Slavs

Celts

Rome

SIBERIA

CENTRAL ASIA

Arctic Circle

▲ A Viking burial ground on Gotland. Some Viking graves were marked with stones in the outlines of ships: this may have been because death was seen as a journey into the unknown, or because ships were so important in Viking life.

TIME LINE

B.C.

c. **25,000** First people in Americas arrive from Asia

c. **10,000** First distinct Native American cultures develop

c. **500s** Celts appear in early Greek histories

c. **100—A.D. 1000** Hopewell Indians build burial mounds in Ohio

58 Julius Caesar begins conquest of Gaul

A.D.

43 Romans invade Britain

c. **200** Germanic peoples begin to spread west and east

c. **400** Slavic peoples begin to emerge as a distinct culture

793 The Viking Age begins

955—1000 Christianity spreads through Denmark, Norway, and Iceland

c. **1600** The use of horses begins to spread among the Plains peoples

· ARCTIC LANDS ·

The lands that lie near the North Pole are cold and bleak. For the people that live there—the Inuit of North America and Greenland and the peoples of northern Russia and Scandinavia—the environment can make life harsh. Farming is impossible, and until recent times people were dependent on hunting and fishing as their only source of food. It is not surprising that animals and weather play an important part in their mythology.

The world of spirits

There is no one supreme god in traditional Inuit mythology: several spirits control the forces of nature. The most important of these are the sea spirit SEDNA, the air spirit Sila, and the Moon spirit TARQEQ.

The world of spirits has power over every part of daily life. In each community, people called shamans have the power to contact the spirits directly. In order to speak with the spirits a shaman first enters a trance. While the shaman's body is unconscious, the soul travels in the spirit world. They might ask for help with the hunt or knowledge to cure someone who is sick.

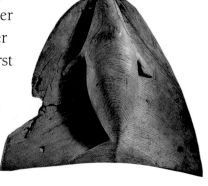

▲ This wooden carving of a whale was lashed to a hunter's boat as a sign of respect for sea animals. The Inuit believe that the hunter and the hunted are equally important.

It is important to keep SEDNA happy, otherwise she will drive the animals away. The Inuit follow certain rules regarding the hunt. In one ceremony, held each year, they throw the bladders of animals they have killed back into the sea.

▶ The Inuit hunt and fish for their food in an icy landscape. Traditionally, they look to the spirits to help them find success in the hunt.

In Inuit mythology, both animals and humans may come back to Earth in some way after they die. An animal may be reborn to be hunted again. After a person dies, part of the soul enters the Underworld or the Sky Realm—worlds that exist below and above the Earth—and part is reborn in a new baby. When the baby is named after the dead person, he or she inherits some of their character traits.

◄ Terrified, SEDNA and her father try to escape from her husband, the storm petrel. The Inuit myth of Sedna, who later became the sea spirit, explains how the sea was filled with seals, fish, and whales. See page 18.

Siberian mythology reflects a special relationship with animals. Like the Inuit, the Siberians traditionally believe that animals have souls and that the hunted is just as important as the hunter. Animals are thought to give themselves willingly to a hunter who respects them.

The brown bear is particularly powerful. He is called the "Lord of the Forest," and can be a dangerous force. At the same time, he has the power to heal injuries. A wound might be healed by being rubbed with bear's fat. Some Siberians say that their people originally came from a half-bear, half-human ancestor.

A Siberian myth exists to explain day and night. It tells how an elk captures the Sun every evening. He carries it away on his antlers, making the world dark. Fortunately, at night a hero reclaims the Sun, and brings it back to Earth in time for morning.

In the prehistoric past, the mammoth was very important to the Siberians. It provided them with meat to eat, bones to make into tools, and skins to make into clothes. Although it is extinct today, the mammoth still appears in Siberian mythology. It is said to have helped make the land with its great tusks and now rules as a master of the Underworld.

The Inuit and Siberian peoples share a traditional belief that several worlds exist, stacked on top of each other. The Earth is in the middle. Good spirits usually live in the upper worlds and evil spirits live in the lower ones. A mythical tree is the path between them. During a trance, a shaman climbs to these other worlds to reach the spirits.

▲ For 700 years
ILMATER floated alone
upon the ocean. Then an
eagle flew over the
horizon. Ilmater formed
a hollow in her lap, and
the eagle made its nest
there, laying seven eggs.
This so excited Ilmater
that she jerked her knees
and the eggs dropped
from her lap and broke
on the surface of the
water. From the
eggshell, the Earth was
formed. The yolks
became the Sun, and the
whites became the Moon
and the stars.

AJYSYT The mother goddess of the Yakut people of Siberia. She lives in Heaven, where she writes the fates of children in a golden book. She is present when a child is born and brings its soul from Heaven to make it a whole person.

ANGAKOQ The title given to an Inuit shaman (someone with a special ability to communicate with the spirit world). Each shaman is watched over by a guardian spirit known as a "tornaq," who may take the form of a human, a stone, or a bear. Through the power of the tornaq, the Angakoq cures illness, controls the weather and the fortunes of the hunters, and keeps the sea spirit SEDNA calm.

BUGA The supreme god of the Tungus people of Siberia. He made the first two people, using earth for the flesh and bones, water for the blood, fire to warm the body, and iron for the heart.

ERLIK The spirit of evil in Siberian and Lapp mythology. He is said to have helped Ulgan, the supreme being, make the world. In other stories Ulgan is said to have made Erlik from mud that he found floating on the ocean. Erlik is lord of the dead and Ulgan is lord of the living.

IGALUK *see* **TARQEQ**

ILMATER The Finnish creator goddess. At the start of time, only she existed, floating on an empty ocean. After 700 years, the Earth and sky were formed from pieces of an eagle's eggs. Ilmater became bored with the Earth as it had no features, so she built mountains and islands, carved valleys, and set rivers running across the land.

JUMALA The Finnish supreme god who made the world and ruled the sky. He is also god of the oak tree. (*See also* UKKO.)

KUL An Arctic water spirit. Though he is sometimes malevolent, the spirit also helps the northern peoples with their fishing. In return, he is offered some of the first fish caught at the start of each season.

PINGA An all-powerful Inuit goddess who is more important than even TARQEQ. She protects all living creatures, controls the hunt, and helps the ANGAKOQ.

SEDNA As a lovely young girl, she wed a storm petrel that had promised her a life of riches. But the bird had lied, and when Sedna's father visited the couple his unhappy daughter asked him to take her home. As they escaped in her father's boat, the petrel chased them, whipping up a storm that threatened to kill them both. Her father flung Sedna overboard but she clung to the boat. To free himself, he cut off her fingers joint by joint. Sedna's fingertips became the smaller seals, her middle joints the bearded seals, and her large joints the walruses. She sank to the bottom of sea, where she now rules Adlivum, the land of the dead. She is so hideous and terrifying that only the ANGAKOQ can bear to look at her.

TARQEQ The Inuit Moon spirit. He is a mighty hunter who lives in the sky and watches over human behavior. The Inuit of Alaska believe he controls the animals.

TULUNGUSAQ The Inuit creator god who took the form of a raven and flew down from his home in the sky. First, he made dry land. Next he made a man, then animals and plants. Finally, he made a woman to be man's companion. Disguised as a human, Tulungusaq taught man and woman how they could benefit by making use of animals, how to make fire, and how to care for children. Tulungusaq is also sometimes known as Raven Father.

UKKO A sky god. He became the Finnish supreme being, replacing JUMALA, whom people had worshiped previously.

ULGAN *see* **ERLIK and YRYN-AI-TOJON**

VAINAMOINEN A sorcerer in Finnish mythology and the hero of the series of stories known as the *Kalevala*. He was the owner of the sampo, a magical mill that granted any wish. Vainamoinen traded the sampo with the Lapplanders in order to marry the Maid of the North. Afterward, he built a harplike musical instrument called the kantle, using a horse's jaw as the frame and hairs from its tail as the strings. He played this to lull the Lapplanders into an enchanted sleep so that he and his brothers could steal the sampo back.

YAMBE-AKKA In Lapp mythology, "the old woman of the dead" and ruler of the Underworld. This was a world similar to the Earth, except that the spirits walked on air. The entrance to the Underworld is said to be found at the mouth of a river flowing into the Arctic ice.

YRYN-AI-TOJON The creator god of the Yakut people of Siberia. (He is known to other Siberian peoples as Ulgan.) In the beginning the world was only ocean. One day Yryn-ai-Tojon came across the spirit of evil, who claimed to live on dry ground beneath the waves. The god persuaded the spirit to bring him up some earth and, spreading it on the water, sat down. The evil spirit tried to break the earth up, but found that the more he stretched it the bigger it became. So the land was made.

▼ *The sorcerer,* VAINAMOINEN, *plays the kantle, a magic musical instrument, so that the Lapplanders fall into an enchanted sleep. Vainamoinen is the main hero of a collection of Finnish stories called the* Kalevala. *This was put together during the 1800s from folktales.*

·NORTH AMERICA·

The native peoples of North America arrived there in small groups over thousands of years. They crossed from Siberia during a time when the sea level was lower, and Alaska and Siberia were joined together where the Bering Strait is now. The people spread south and east across the continent, and each community adapted to suit the type of environment in which it settled.

Hundreds of cultures with different languages and ways of life were established. Among such a wide range of communities, the peoples' beliefs were as varied as their lifestyles. But some themes do appear in most or all of the mythologies. Myths that explain how the world was made and where people came from are common. Also, many communities tell the story of a hero who gave human beings their first laws or set up basic social institutions. Myths were frequently told both to entertain people and to teach them the right way to behave.

Native Americans did not write their myths down, but passed them on by word of mouth (the oral tradition). Myths were passed on by members of the community who were particularly good storytellers and had specially trained memories.

The Great Spirit

Most Native Americans believed in a GREAT SPIRIT—an especially powerful god who made the world, or at least inspired its creation. People gave him different names. The Selish called him AMOTKEN; the Algonquin, GITCHE MANITOU.

The Great Spirit is a vague figure who is surrounded by better defined beings such as MOTHER EARTH or FATHER SKY. These were responsible for the specific details of creation.

The most common creator figure is the Earth Diver. Before the world began, he dived into the sea and brought back mud, which became the Earth. In many myths the Earth is said to rest on the back of a turtle.

Arctic and sub-Arctic

Northwest Coast

Far west
(including California)

Southwest

Plateau

Great Basin

Southeast

Plains

Eastern
Woodlands

◄ *The hundreds of different Native American communties are loosely grouped together in "culture areas." Communities in the same group led a similar way of life.*

▲ *A shaman of the Haida peoples of the Northwest Coast used a rattle like this in rituals to help him contact spirits or heal the sick.*

Usually, one or more creator gods are said to have made the first people. Many myths tell how people climbed up onto Earth from an underground cave, as happens in the Pueblo story of MASEWI AND OYOYEWA.

Often, a hero leads the first people on a journey through several tests; along the way he teaches them how to organize their society properly and how they should behave. Some peoples believe that the first ancestor was a woman, such as the Iroquois ancestor, ATAENSIC.

▶ *Dancers in the winter ceremony of the Kwakiutl (Northwest Coast) wear masks that show animals important to the mythology of their community.*

Animals play an important part in Native American mythology. It is said that a long time ago, animals could change to a human shape if they wished. Among the peoples of the Northwest Coast, some groups believe that families, or clans, were originally founded by animals who took on a human shape. These animals are now the special symbols, or "totems," of each clan.

Images of the mythical animal are carved on wooden totem poles. These show a clan's status in their community or sometimes tell the family's history in pictures. They are placed at the entrance to a village, or by the grave of a dead chief, or sometimes outside a clan house.

In Native American mythology direct contact with the spirits and gods is very important. Most people believed in a guardian spirit, who acted as a kind of spirit helper. It watched over an individual and guided them through their life.

In their early teens, boys—and in some cases girls—would set out on a vision quest. This involved prayer and fasting in a remote place in an attempt to find their personal guardian spirit. Some youths wounded themselves to help bring about the vision. The spirit often took the form of a bird or animal.

▶ *The Sun Dance of the Lakota, drawn on the hide of a bison. Dancers performed around a pole that stood for the link between the Earth, sky, and Underworld. With their community gathered around them in a large circle, the dancers continued until they entered a vision trance and collapsed from exhaustion.*

▼ *The Plains peoples performed buffalo dances to ensure a good supply of animals for food and skins.*

Although anyone could contact the spirit world, only certain individuals became shamans—people who were believed to have a particularly powerful link with the spirits. A shaman's position in the community often began with a serious illness in youth. During this ordeal the shaman was visited by the spirits and given sacred knowledge.

The shaman's relationship with the spirit world was used to help the community in various ways. For instance, a shaman helped find animals to hunt. A shaman also had powers to heal the sick. By entering a trance, the shaman would visit the spirit world to search for a cure.

Native Americans held many different kinds of ceremonies that frequently involved music and dancing. Often, the ceremonies were linked with food. For example, the Green Corn Dance of the Eastern Woodlands offered thanks for a good harvest.

Among the peoples of the Plains area, the Sun was the major figure in their creation myth, and the most important ceremony was the Sun Dance, held once a year.

At first, the ceremony was held to thank the Sun for his favors. Individuals also used the dance to contact the spirits and gain power from them. Some people injured themselves deliberately as part of the dance, and this was seen as a way of setting themselves free of ignorance. Today, the dance has different meanings to each of the groups that perform it.

In the Southwest, dry (or "sand") paintings play an important part in healing ceremonies. They are based on traditional designs and painted from memory. Every detail must be exactly as originally laid down, or the cure will not work.

Native American myths about an afterlife are few. They generally describe a place similar to the Earth, but where there is plenty of all the good things in life, especially game. Among the Plains tribes this was known as the Happy Hunting Ground.

▼ *A sacred pipe made during the 1800s by a member of the Sioux.*

Another common ceremony found in the Plains and Woodlands was the ritual of smoking the sacred pipe. This symbolized the link between the family, the community and the universe. The Lakota myth of the origin of the sacred pipe tells how it was presented to a chief by a woman who then changed into a buffalo. Sacred pipes were carved with symbols that stood for creation and the owner's personal guardian spirits and visions.

In the Southwest, sacred ceremonies were held in underground rooms called kivas. The kiva represents Mother Earth. A hole in its floor represents SHIPAP, the place from which people entered the world. A ladder through a hole in the top of the room leads to the world above. Prayers are offered before the kiva "altar," accompanied by feathered prayer sticks and other objects.

The Hopi of the Southwest believe that after death the soul of a good person becomes a spirit called a KACHINA. For half the year kachinas live in the spirit world, but from winter to midsummer they return to the Hopi. During this time they are symbolized by dancers who wear painted masks. There are over 300 kachinas, and each has a distinct personality and mask. The Hopi dedicate services to the kachinas to ensure a good harvest.

▼ *According to legend,* ATOTAROH *had magic powers that he used to send a giant white bird to kill the daughter of* HIAWATHA. *Despite this, Hiawatha continued with his plan to unite the five Iroquois nations. When Atotaroh at last came over to his side, Hiawatha combed the snakes from Atotaroh's hair to show that he had changed from evil to good.*

AMOTKEN The creator god of the Selish people of the Northwest Coast. Amotken is a very old, wise, and kind man who watches over the well-being of human beings. He created Heaven (where he lives alone), Earth, and the Underworld—all three supported on a gigantic post.

■

ASGAYA GIGAGEI Originally the thunder god of the Cherokee of the Eastern Woodlands, but now associated more with healing. A shaman who is attempting to cure someone's sickness will call on Asgaya Gigagei for help.

■

ATAENSIC The first ancestor of the Iroquois and Huron peoples of the Eastern Woodlands. She was the child of the Sky People—gods who came down to Earth. She died giving birth to twin sons, HAHGWEHDIYU AND HAHGWEHDAETGAH, and her body was used by Hahgwehdiyu to create the Earth. She is considered both Sky Woman and MOTHER EARTH.

■

ATIUS TIRAWA *see* **TIRAWA**

■

ATOTAROH A legendary Mohawk shaman and war chief. His head was covered in snakes and he was so evil that even his presence caused birds to fall from the sky. The hero HIAWATHA planned to bring the five Iroquois peoples, including the Mohawks, together in a peaceful union. At first Atotaroh was violently against this and did what he could to prevent it, but in the end he changed his mind. Atotaroh later became leader of the league of the five Iroquois nations.

AWONAWILONA The creator god of the Zuni, who can be either a woman or a man, and is known as the "All-container." FATHER SKY and MOTHER EARTH were made from mist and streams that issued from Awonawilona's body. Inside Mother Earth were four wombs containing creatures, including POSHAIYANGKYO, the first man.

■

COYOTE A trickster figure of the peoples of the Southwest, West, and Plains. He is sly, mischievous, and destructive, and likes causing chaos in the world. A myth of the Maidu people of California tells how WONOMI made the first people. Coyote soon grew bored watching their happy, easy life. To make things more "interesting," he gave to humankind sickness, sorrow, and death. As luck would have it, the first person to die was Coyote's own son, bitten by Coyote's companion, Rattlesnake.

■

DZELARHONS A legendary woman who came to marry Kaiti, the bear god of the people of the Northwest Coast. From the start of the marriage, her husband did not treat Dzelarhons as he should, and when her uncle Githawn learned of this he made war upon Kaiti. Dzelarhons disappeared and when Githawn searched for her all he could find was a stone statue.

■

DZOAVITS A giant ogre in Shoshone mythology who kidnapped Dove's two children. Eagle and Crane helped Dove to rescue them, but as they escaped the ogre chased after them. They were saved by Badger, who dug two holes. Dove and his children hid in one, and when Dzoavits arrived demanding to know where they were, Badger pointed to the second hole. As the ogre crawled in, Badger plugged the hole with a stone.

ENIGORIO AND ENIGONHAHETGEA Two spirits of the Iroquois and other Northeastern Woodland peoples whose names mean "good mind" and "bad mind." Enigorio made the first people and filled the Earth with animals and plants for them. Enigonhahetgea made reptiles to injure people and changed the Earth's landscape, adding mountains, waterfalls, and other hazards. Then Enigonhahetgea tried to make people of his own from clay. His first efforts failed, but in a second attempt he was helped by Enigorio, who gave the clay figures living souls.

■

ENUMCLAW AND KAPOONIS The thunder and lightning spirits of the Chinook, Columbia, Spokane, and other peoples of the Northwest. They were two brothers who set out to find guardian spirits to teach them the ways of the shamans. Kapoonis found a fire spirit, who taught him to produce lightning, and Enumclaw became expert at stone throwing. FATHER SKY was worried about their new powers, so he made them part of the spirit world themselves, as lightning and thunder.

ESTSANATLEHI The chief goddess of the Navajo people of the Southwest. She is the wife of TSOHANOAI, the Sun god, and lives alone in a house that floats on the western waters. Tsohanoai meets her there every evening as he sets. One day, feeling lonely, she created men and women from small pieces of her own skin. When winter arrives she grows old, but with the spring she becomes young again.

■

FATHER SKY A universal creator god, known by different names among the various Native American cultures.

■

GA-GAAH To the Iroquois, a wise crow who flew to Earth from the kingdom of the Sun, bringing a kernel of corn. The creator god, HAHGWEHDIYU, planted the kernel in MOTHER EARTH, giving the gift of maize to human beings.

■

GITCHE MANITOU The supreme god of the Algonquin peoples of the Northeast Woodlands. He is the master creator who made (or ordered to be made) the Earth, humans, animals, and plants.

▲ DZELARHONS *arrived by sea when she came to marry the bear god Kaiti. She is said to have led six canoes, filled with enough people to start a new community.*

As a newborn baby, ESTSANATLEHI was found on a mountain by the first man and woman. They fed her pollen that the Sun god, TSOHANOAI, gave to them, and she grew into a woman in only 18 days.

▲ A Sioux chief wearing the feathered war bonnet. In Sioux myth, ICTINIKE taught the customs of war.

Henry Longfellow's famous poem *The Song of Hiawatha* was written in the 1800s. It puts the hero at the center of a number of Algonquin legends. In fact, HIAWATHA was an Iroquois leader.

GLOOSKAP A creator god of the peoples of the Northeast Woodlands. He is on the side of good and competes with his evil twin brother, Malsum. Their mother died when Malsum was born out of her armpit. Glooskap used her dead body to form the Earth. Then he fired arrows at ash trees, and people emerged from the bark. He taught them the civilized arts, but they were so ungrateful that Glooskap decided to leave the Earth and sailed away in his canoe. He is expected to return some day.

GREAT SPIRIT The supreme god of most Native American peoples, known by various names. (*See* GITCHE MANITOU, MAHEO, TIRAWA, and WAKAN TANKA.)

HAHGWEHDIYU AND HAHGWEHDAETGAH Iroquois creator gods and the twin sons of ATAENSIC, the Sky Woman. Hahgwehdiyu stands for good and his brother for evil. When their mother died Hahgwehdiyu used her body to make the Earth fertile. His brother challenged Hahgwehdiyu's power of goodness. They fought a duel and when Hahgwehdaetgah lost, evil was banished to the Underworld.

HIAWATHA An Onondaga Iroquois hero, leader, and wise man. He is said to have been the founder, or cofounder with Deganawida, of the League of Iroquois, a confederacy of the five Iroquois peoples (Mohawk, Oneida, Onondaga, Cayuga, and Seneca). He is also credited with having taught his people farming, navigation, medicine, and the arts.

HISAKITAIMISI The supreme god of the Creek peoples from the Eastern Woodlands. His name means "Master of breath." He is also known as the Sun god, Ibofanga, meaning "He who sits above."

ICTINIKE A war god whose father was the Iowa Sun god. He invented lies, and his adventures usually involve deceit, cunning, and treachery. Even his own father tired of this and threw him out of Heaven. It is said that Ictinike taught the Sioux and many other Plains peoples the customs of war.

IOSKEHA The guardian spirit of the Huron, Mohawk, and Tuscarora. His twin brother, Tawiscara, was the spirit of evil. The brothers fought for supremacy: Ioskeha was armed with staghorns, but Tawiscara had only a wild rose. When Ioskeha won, Tawiscara was forced to keep his evildoing within bounds.

IYATIKU The corn goddess of the Keresan Pueblo peoples of the Southwest. She lives in an underground realm called SHIPAP. Babies are born in Shipap and people return there when they die.

KACHINA   The name given to the spirits of ancestors by the Pueblo peoples.

◾

KICI MANITU   see GITCHE MANITOU

◾

KUMUSH   The creator god of the Modoc people of northern California. With his daughter he visited the spirits in the Underworld. At night the spirits sang and danced, but during the day they became dry bones. Kumush brought a great basket of bones back up to Earth and used them to create the various peoples. He and his daughter live in a house in the sky.

▼ *In Native American mythology, the first people are often said to have been led up to Earth from underground.*

▲ *At Pueblo festivals masked dancers played the parts of KACHINA spirits. Kachinas were associated with all parts of daily life.*

MAHEO   The supreme god or GREAT SPIRIT of the Cheyenne peoples of the Plains. At the start of time, nothing existed until Maheo made the ocean, the water animals, and birds. After a while the birds grew tired of flying all the time and searched for land but failed to find anywhere dry to rest.

Finally, the coot flew back with a ball of mud, which he gave to Maheo. The god rolled the mud around in his palm, until it grew so big that only Grandmother Turtle was able to support it on her back. This was how the Earth began.

◾

MASEWI AND OYOYEWA   Twin brothers and war spirits who in Pueblo mythology were sent by their mother to put the Sun in the sky and decide to which clan people should belong.

The Hopi people of the Southwest tell myths about Masau'u, the fire god. He was the caretaker of the Fourth World (the "World Complete," or Earth), into which mankind came after a long journey through SIPAPU.

▼ When the first woman asked NAPI if people would live forever, he threw a piece of wood into a river, declaring that if it floated, death would last only four days; if it sank, death would be final. The wood floated. The woman picked up a stone, saying "if the stone floats we will live forever; if it sinks, we will die." The stone sank and now death is final.

MOTHER EARTH A universal creator goddess, known by different names among the various peoples. She is also the womb of the Earth (SHIPAP), out of which humankind is led, in some myths by the Corn Mother or Spider Woman, in others by twin brothers or a hero figure. (*See* ATAENSIC, AWONAWILONA, IYATIKU, and MASEWI AND OYOYEWA.)

NANABOZHO A trickster figure to the Algonquins of the Northwest Woodlands. He is also known as Nanabush. He lived with his younger brother until the brother was drowned by jealous spirits. In a fit of fury, Nanabozho attacked the murderers until they revealed to him the details of a sacred ceremony, called the Mide. The ceremony was so powerful that the drowned brother was raised from the dead and appointed chief of the Underworld.

NAPI The creator god of the Blackfoot of the Plains whose name means "old man." Having made the world and the first man and woman from clay, he is said to have withdrawn into the mountains, promising to return at some time in the future. Meanwhile, he has been replaced by NATOS, the Sun god. In other stories, Napi is said to be a trickster god capable of great mischief, and even malevolence, toward humankind.

NATOS The Blackfoot Sun god and supreme being. His wife is Kokomikeis, the Moon goddess. Their children were the stars, until the pelicans killed all of them except Apisuahts, the morning star.

NAYENEZGANI AND TOBADZISTSINI War gods and brothers in Navajo mythology, whose parents are TSOHANOAI and ESTSANATLEHI. The brothers patrol the world, protecting humankind against evil. Tsohanoai gave them powerful weapons, including a chain-lightning arrow, a sheet-lightning arrow, a sunbeam arrow, and a rainbow arrow. They used these to defeat Yeitso, the scaly one, Teelget, a four-footed beast with deer horns; and the Tsenahale, huge eaglelike birds with fearsome talons.

POSHAIYANGKYO The wise leader and founder of the Zuni, a Pueblo people of the Southwest. He was the first to find a passageway leading up from and out of MOTHER EARTH. He prayed for help from AWONAWILONA to bring forth the creatures still below in the womb of the Earth. He sent MASEWI AND OYOYEWA to lead the creatures to the present world.

RAVEN According to the Haida of the Northwest Coast, a creator figure. Before the world began, Raven was thrown out of Heaven. At first, the bird did not know what to do; but then, by flapping his wings he made land rise from the first sea. Later, he made people from clamshells and stole the Sun from Heaven to bring light to the world. Raven is also seen as a trickster figure in the Northwest; there are many stories about him.

SHIPAP The name given to the womb of the Earth by the Pueblo peoples of the Southwest. (*See also* SIPAPU.)

SIPAPU   The womb of the Earth according to the Hopi peoples of the Southwest. The Hopi ancestors had to pass through the three underground worlds of Sipapu before reaching the Fourth World where people live today. The First World was pure, but the first people corrupted it with war until it was destroyed by fire. For the same reason, the Second World was destroyed by ice, and the Third World by floods. Finally, two brothers led the people into the present Fourth World.

■

THUNDERBIRD   The spirit of thunder, a figure known among peoples throughout North America. He appears on Earth as a giant eaglelike bird with eyes that flash lightning and whose wingbeats cause thunderclaps. He has awesome powers and is constantly struggling against evil.

TIRAWA   The supreme god of the Plains Pawnee. He is known as the "arch of Heaven." He decided the paths that the Sun, Moon, and stars should take in the sky and gave each of them part of his power. Tirawa then ordered the Sun and Moon to marry, and their child was the first man; the morning star and evening star also married on Tirawa's instruction, and their child was the first woman. Tirawa is also known as Atius Tirawa.

■

TONENILI   The Navajo rain god. His name means "water sprinkler," and he is shown carrying a water pot. Tonenili enjoys playing practical jokes on humankind, but these are never harmful. With the fire god, Hastsezini, he rescued the first Navajo from Ticholtsodi, the water monster.

▲ TIRAWA *decided on the position that the Sun, Moon, and stars should take in the sky.*

THUNDERBIRD's character varies. To the Lakota he is an assistant to FATHER SKY. In the Northwest he is the chief sky god and preys on whales; to the Iroquois he takes human shape as Hino, the thunder spirit. Western peoples believe in four thunderbirds, one for each quarter of the world.

The Quinault peoples tell myths of the trickster creator god Kwatee. At first, the world was filled with giant animals, such as Ant, Spider, Beaver, and Fox. They challenged Kwatee when he began to prepare the Earth for humans, so he changed them into ordinary animals. Then, he rubbed his hands all over his body, making little balls of sweat and dirt, and from these he created the first people.

TSOHANOAI The Navajo Sun god and husband of ESTSANATLEHI. He carries the Sun across the sky on his back and at night hangs it on the west wall of his house. His sons are NAYENEZGANI AND TOBADZISTSINI, to whom he gave magic weapons to fight the Anaye, evil monster gods who devoured men.

■

WAKAN TANKA The GREAT SPIRIT and creator god of the Lakota of the Plains. He is the "Great Mystery," whose spirit was in the first god, Inyan (Rock). In the beginning, nothing else existed except Han (Black of Darkness). From his own blood, Inyan created the goddess Maka (the Earth) and the blue waters. From the waters he made the god Skan (the sky). Skan then brought light to the world by creating the god Wi (the Sun). Inyan, Maka, Skan and Wi then declared Wakan Tanka to be the supreme god.

WAKONDA The "Great Mystery" or "Power Above" of the Plains Sioux. Wakonda is the source of all power and wisdom in the world and enlightens the holy men and healers known as medicine men.

■

WISAKEDJAK One of the names of the trickster god among the peoples of the Eastern Woodlands. He was known as "Whisky Jack" in English.

■

WISHPOOSH A beaver monster that prevented the Nez Percés of the northern plains and plateau from fishing. They asked COYOTE for help, and he stabbed the beaver with a huge spear. But it escaped, with Coyote still clinging to the spear. Coyote turned into a fir branch, which the beaver swallowed, whereupon Coyote changed back and stabbed the beaver in the heart. From the corpse Coyote created the peoples of the Northwest Coast.

TRICKSTER

A trickster is a supernatural being and a hero who, through his cunning, often brings some form of good to his people; sometimes the trickster is a creator god. At the same time, he often cannot tell the difference between good and evil.

The trickster stands for the forces of mischief and destruction, but he can also represent less harmful horseplay, crafty trickery, or even bungling behavior. In his more sinister form, he enjoys bringing chaos and disorder to the world.

Tricksters in Native American myth include Great Hare or Rabbit, Racoon, or other animals among the woodland peoples of the Northeast and Southeast; COYOTE (shown here being pulled out to sea by WISHPOOSH) in the Southwest, West, and Plains; and RAVEN, Bluejay, or Mink among the Northwest Coast peoples.

WONOMI The Sky Father and supreme god of the Maidu people of California. He made the world and the natural elements and created humankind. He was challenged by his arch rival, COYOTE, who won by using trickery. While Coyote rules on Earth, Wonomi remains concerned for people, who can still go to Wonomi's realm above the clouds after death.

■

YANAULUHA The great medicine man of the Zuni people of the Southwest. Because they had been living underground, when the first men and women emerged from SIPAPU they were black and scaly, with tails, owl's eyes, large ears, and webbed feet. Yanauluha, who had brought water, plant seeds, and a staff that had the power of life, changed them by teaching them farming and how to keep order in their community.

■

YADILYIL In Navajo myth, the "Upper Darkness," who with Naestan ("Horizontal Woman") created ESTSANATHLEHI from a black cloud covering a mountaintop.

YEI, THE Navajo gods who played an important role in the creation of the world. They are sometimes impersonated during curing ceremonies by people wearing masks. The Yei leader is Talking God. He once made a Navajo girl pregnant. She gave birth to twin boys, who were later crushed in a terrible rockfall. One boy was made blind and the other lame. They became a burden to their family and were driven from home. The twins appealed to the Yei, who prepared a curing ceremony. The twins were fully restored and on returning home taught their people the ceremony. Soon after, they left to become the guardian spirits of thunderstorms and animals.

■

YOLKAI ESTAN A Navajo sea goddess known as "White Shell Woman." She is the sister of ESTSANATLEHI.

▲ *The first people came from underground and were black and scaly.* YANAULUHA *taught them the art of growing plants and how to adapt to life on the Earth's surface.*

· THE CELTS AND THE SLAVS ·

The myths of the Celtic and Slavic peoples are two of the three main groups in northern European mythology. The third group, the Norse, is discussed on pages 42–53. Each group of myths is different, but there is much overlap between the Celtic and Nordic gods, and scholars believe that elements of the myths of all three came from western Asia.

The Celts were an ancient people who lived in central Europe before gradually spreading across the continent. Some settled in France, Portugal, Spain, and the British Isles. Others moved east, toward Turkey. The Celtic peoples are linked together because they spoke languages that are alike; but at no time did they form a single nation under one leader, nor did they all worship the same gods.

Between about 300 B.C. and A.D. 100, the Romans conquered much of Europe. The only Celts to keep their own culture were those in the British Isles and the Gauls in northern France.

▼ *The Celts had no writing. Their myths, laws, and religious rituals were passed on by word of mouth, probably by druids (priests) and bards (skilled musicians and storytellers). Here, the tale of the adventures of a great hero is accompanied by music.*

▲ *The god* CERNUNNOS *appears on the Gundestrup cauldron surrounded by beasts and dragonlike creatures.*

Celtic gods

The Celts did not write their mythology down, but passed it on by word of mouth. So it is not easy to know for sure who their gods were. Information about ancient Celtic gods comes mostly from the Romans.

The Romans sometimes called Celtic gods by Roman names because they were like Roman gods. For example, Julius Caesar describes a god called Lugus as the greatest of the Celtic gods. This was probably the Irish god LUGH, who invented all the crafts. Caesar links Lugus with Mercury, the Roman god of skill and trade.

► *A scene from the Welsh* Mabinogion, *in which a giant brings the Irish king Matholowch a magic cauldron.*

Most Celtic gods appear to have been figures that were local to the community. Some of the most ancient Celtic gods were Lugus; DAGHDA, "the good god" or "mighty one of great knowledge;" CERNUNNOS, "the horned one;" DONAR (the god of thunder); and WODAN (the god of the Underworld).

None of the Celtic myths from the continent of Europe have survived as whole stories. Only snatches remain. We know far more about the Celtic myths from Ireland and Wales, which have been preserved in manuscripts from the 700s and 1300s.

The *Mabinogion* is an important collection of stories from Welsh mythology, written down in the 1800s. In its first four books it tells the mythical history of early Britain. The collection contains 11 books in all.

Celtic peoples believed that those who died went to an "Otherworld," found in the west, which could be entered through caves or lakes. Reaching this world involved a dangerous journey, but the people who live there are happy forever.

Much Irish mythology is contained in four important cycles, or series, of connected stories. The first cycle tells how five races of supernatural people (including the TUATHA DE DANAAN) battled to rule Ireland. The second cycle relates the adventures of CU CHULAINN, "the champion of all Ireland," who fought the wicked MEDHBHA. The adventures of legendary kings appear in the third cycle; the hero FINN MAC COOL and his brave warriors are the subjects of the fourth.

The theme of heroes who set out on great voyages and carry out difficult tasks is found in the best known Welsh myths, which concern King ARTHUR and his knights. Their sacred mission was to discover the Holy Grail, the cup that Jesus Christ used at the Last Supper. The hero king, Arthur, is an example of a common belief in leaders who, despite being killed or mortally wounded in battle, will return to defend their people when called upon in extreme need in the future. Arthur is said to have been taken by fairies to Avalon, where he waits to return one day.

Slavic mythology

While Celtic myths are handed down mainly from western Europe, the myths from central and eastern Europe are part of Slavic mythology.

The Slavs include many peoples, ranging from Russia to Macedonia. Each has its own language and customs, but they have many myths in common.

Early Slavic myths were not written down. Writing was adopted when Christianity arrived in the 800s and 900s. After people became Christian, the old gods were often condemned.

▼ *King* ARTHUR *owned the magical sword Excalibur, which was given to him by the Lady of the Lake. It is said that after being terribly wounded during his final battle, Arthur handed Excalibur to the knight Bedivere. He asked the knight to take the sword and cast it into a lake. At first Bedivere could not bring himself to do it, but eventually he obeyed. An arm rose from the water and caught Excalibur, shook it three times, and carried it beneath the surface.*

Many of the gods in Slavic myths represent the forces of nature. Dazhbog, for example, is god of the Sun, while his brother SVAROZHICH is the god of fire. PERUNU is god of thunder.

We know little about how these gods were worshiped. Apparently, shamans (people who enter a trance to communicate with the spirits) played an important part in contacting the spirit world, or Other World, as it was known.

In some stories the Other World is found beyond thick forests on the other side of a fiery river. In other myths it is above, below, or beyond the sea and Earth. The Slavs saw the Earth itself as an island floating in a great ocean. Like the Norse myth of Yggdrasil (*see page* 53), they believed in a World Tree that links the different realms. Its roots reach the land of the dead and its branches reach the heavens.

The Slavic god Byelobog, or the "white god," stands for all goodness, life and light. He brings wealth and fertility and helps with the harvest. His opposite is Chernobog, or the "black god," who is the epitome of evil, death, and darkness.

▶ *The* DOMOVOI *is a household spirit who lives near the kitchen stove. Generally he is invisible, but he is said to be a hairy, gray-bearded man. He is normally good-tempered, but if a family does not leave his favorite food out at night he smashes crockery and upsets the animals.*

The Slavs believed that the power of light battled against the destructive power of darkness. People called on the good powers to protect them against the force of evil. When people became Christian, they linked the good powers with the Church.

Every home was watched over by dead ancestors, and the Slavs practiced elaborate ceremonies to honor dead relatives. Several times a year, on fixed days, people feasted beside the graves, and food was left for the dead person's spirit to feast on afterward.

Slavs believed in many different spirits. There were spirits of the home, called the DOMOVOI, and of the farmhouse and its different buildings, the DVOROVOI and the OVINNIK.

Other spirits represented the soul of someone who had died young. Finally there were spiteful spirits whose role was to bring people bad luck, or even just play tricks on them. Among these were WEREWOLVES AND VAMPIRES, and among the East Slavs, the fearsome forest spirit known as LESHII.

The most important adventure of ARTHUR and the Knights of the Round Table was the quest for the Holy Grail, the cup from which Christ drank at the Last Supper. Joseph of Arimathea brought the Grail to England, where it was lost until found by GALAHAD.

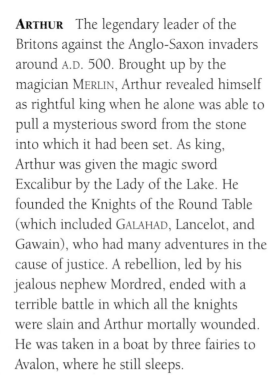

▼ BABA IAGA *lives deep in the forest, in a hut that stands on chicken legs and is surrounded by a fence of bones. It is said that she guards the gate to the Other World.*

ARTHUR The legendary leader of the Britons against the Anglo-Saxon invaders around A.D. 500. Brought up by the magician MERLIN, Arthur revealed himself as rightful king when he alone was able to pull a mysterious sword from the stone into which it had been set. As king, Arthur was given the magic sword Excalibur by the Lady of the Lake. He founded the Knights of the Round Table (which included GALAHAD, Lancelot, and Gawain), who had many adventures in the cause of justice. A rebellion, led by his jealous nephew Mordred, ended with a terrible battle in which all the knights were slain and Arthur mortally wounded. He was taken in a boat by three fairies to Avalon, where he still sleeps.

BABA IAGA A powerful witch in Slavic mythology. She has power over animals and birds, and over day and night. She is an ugly hag, so skinny that she looks like a skeleton with sharp teeth. Sometimes she is known as "Bonylegs." She travels in a mortar, propelling herself with a pestle, and sweeps away her tracks with a broom.

BEOWULF A legendary Anglo-Saxon hero of immense strength, from the land of the Geats in southern Sweden. He journeyed to Denmark to help King Hrothgar rid his realm of the man-eating monster Grendel. No weapon could kill the monster, so Beowulf held it in a mighty embrace and crushed the creature to death. When he was old, his kingdom was devastated by a dragon. Beowulf and the young chieftain Wiglaf destroyed the dragon, but Beowulf was wounded and died.

BRAN A legendary king of Britain, also known as Bran the Blessed, and a man of enormous size. After being severely wounded in battle, he ordered his followers to cut off his head and bury it at the White Mount, later the site of the Tower of London, where it would protect Britain against invasion. In Irish legend, Bran is a hero who, with 26 warriors, sailed to a magical place called the Otherworld. They thought that their adventures had lasted a year, but in fact centuries had gone by. When they returned to Ireland, Bran was remembered only as a voyager hero in legends.

BRIGHID A Celtic goddess of poetry, mystery, and magic arts. She was the daughter of DAGHDA, and had two sisters, also called Brighid. One was a goddess of healing; the other, goddess of metalcraft.

CERNUNNOS The "horned one" or antlered god of Celtic mythology. He is lord of all animals, as well as a fertility god connected with the return of spring and the provision of a plentiful supply of food.

CU CHULAINN A legendary Irish hero and the son of the Sun god, LUGH. He defended Ulster against the army of MEDHBHA, queen of Connacht, who was trying to steal the Brown Bull of Cooley from its owner. An old curse brought a great sickness upon the warriors of Ulster. Only Cu Chulainn and his mortal father were unaffected and well enough to fight. Alone they took on the entire forces of Connacht and defeated them.

Cu Chulainn later met his death from a magic spear made by the children of a warrior slain by the hero.

DAGHDA The ancient Celtic god of life and death, known as the "good god," and an early chief of the TUATHA DE DANAAN. He controls the weather and crops and is skilled in magic. Daghda is also called "mighty one of great knowledge" because he possesses all wisdom.

DANAAN (DANA, DANU, DONU) The mother of the Irish gods and a special goddess of the TUATHA DE DANAAN, the earliest people to conquer Ireland. She is a Celtic goddess of prosperity and plenty.

DIAN CECHT The divine healer in Irish mythology. He sings magic spells over a well, and mortally wounded or dead warriors are brought back to life when they are bathed in its waters.

DOMOVOI Spirits of the home in Slavic mythology. They are rarely seen, being active only at night, but are said to look like gray-bearded old men covered from head to toe with tangled hair. The Slavic peoples treat the domovoi with great respect and leave out the finest food and drink as offerings for them.

DONAR The northern European god of thunder. Like the Slavic god PERUNU, he is associated with the great oak forests, and carries an ax, the symbol of lightning. He is linked with the Norse god Thor and called Thunor by the Anglo-Saxons.

DRUIDS The sacred priests, teachers, and wise men of the Celts whose patron was DAGHDA. The druids met in groves of oak trees, where they collected mistletoe to use in their ceremonies.

▲ *For four days* CU CHULAINN *fought his foster brother, Fer Diadh, in single combat, as* MEDHBHA *watched from her horse. Fer Diadh was the greatest of the warriors chosen by Medhbha to fight Cu Chulainn in the war over the Brown Bull of Cooley.*

The touch of a hairy DOMOVOI brings good luck to the household, but a cold, hard touch foretells death or ill-fortune. When a family moves, special rituals ensure that the domovoi moves too.

▲ FINN MAC COOL was called Demhne as a boy. The name Finn was given to him by his tutor, Finn the Poet, after the boy had burned his thumb on the Salmon of Knowledge. From that time on, whenever Finn Mac Cool put his thumb into his mouth and sang certain words, anything he needed to know was made clear to him.

FINN MAC COOL One of the most important figures in Irish mythology. He was the legendary leader of a band of warrior-heroes called the Fianna, which roamed Ireland hunting, wooing, and fighting. Finn is said not to be dead but to be sleeping in a cave, and will rise again when Ireland is in great peril.

As a boy, Finn was taught by a poet who had waited seven years for the arrival of the Salmon of Knowledge. When at last the salmon was caught, the poet told his pupil to cook the fish, but on no account to eat it, since he wanted to keep its knowledge for himself.

As Finn cooked the salmon, he burned his thumb, and put it into his mouth to ease the pain. The poet realized then that it was not his but the boy's destiny to eat the salmon, and Finn came to possess all knowledge.

GALAHAD In the legend of ARTHUR, he was the purest and most noble knight of the Round Table and son of Sir Lancelot. One seat at the Round Table, the Siege Perilous, was kept empty for the knight that was destined to find the Holy Grail—the cup used by Christ at the Last Supper. The ground would open up and swallow less worthy men who took this seat. Only Galahad proved worthy enough to sit there unharmed, and he alone succeeded in finding the Holy Grail.

■

GOIBHNIU, LUCHTA, AND CREIDHNE The three Irish craftsmen gods who provided the TUATHA DE DANAAN with weapons. Goibhniu is the host at the Otherworld Feast, where he serves a magic potion that makes those who drink it immortal.

■

KIKIMORA Female house spirits in Russian mythology. Like the DOMOVOI, they are rarely seen but are thought to be small with long hair. They are sometimes said to be married to the domovoi.

■

LER (LIR) A Celtic sea god and one of the TUATHA DE DANAAN. His four children were changed into swans by Aoife, their jealous stepmother. Ler tried to change his children back from swans, but Aoife's magic was too strong. It took 900 years for the spell to be lifted, by which time his children had grown old and withered.

■

LUGH A Celtic Sun god and the father of the hero, CU CHULAINN. Lugh is a master craftsman and an expert warrior with the spear and the sling. His skill with these weapons gave the TUATHA DE DANAAN victory over their enemies, the Formorii, and Lugh was made king. He spared the Formorii leader, who in return taught the Tuatha the secrets of farming.

MABINOGI A legendary family in Wales. The family tree had four main branches, and the adventures of each have been collected together to form an epic series of myths called the *Mabinogion*. The most famous of these include stories of BRAN and Don (who may be the Welsh equivalent of DANAAN).

■

MAKOSH (MOKOSH) A fertility goddess, known only to the eastern Slavs. She is associated with water and the plentiful supply of food.

■

MEDHBHA The legendary queen of Connacht. Medhbha is said to have been the wife of nine Irish kings: only her partner could hold the throne.
One story about her tells how she was jealous of her husband, who owned the great White-Horned Bull. Medhbha decided that she must have the equally fine Brown Bull of Cooley and sent her army to steal it from Ulster. When her forces were defeated by CU CHULAINN, Medhbha taught witchcraft to the children of a slain Connacht warrior. They made three magic spears, one of which killed Cu Chulainn.

MERLIN In Welsh legend he was known as Myrddin and could see into the future. The terror of battle made him mad, and he fled into a forest where he lived like a wild man.

Merlin is better known in the legend of ARTHUR, as a magician, enchanter, and wise man. He brought together Arthur's parents, Uther Pendragon and Igraine, and taught and prepared the boy for his destiny as king of the Britons. When Arthur came to the throne, he often used Merlin as his messenger, since the magician could take any shape.

Merlin used his powers to protect Arthur, but the old magician had a weakness for women and later revealed the secrets of his magic to the Lady of the Lake. She used the magic to entangle Merlin forever within the branches of a hawthorn tree.

■

NEHALENNIA A fertility goddess in Germanic mythology worshiped by peoples on the coast of Holland.

The people of ancient Denmark used to worship Nerthus, a fertility goddess. They carried her image around the countryside in a wagon to make the crops grow well.

▼ MERLIN *is said to have created the Round Table, at which the knights of King* ARTHUR *sat. The circular shape of the table meant that no one knight felt less or more important than another.*

▲ PERUNU *is said to blaze across the sky in a fiery chariot pulled by a billy goat.*

N UADHU AIRGEDLAMH means "Nuadhu of the silver hand." His right arm was cut off in battle. Since a blemished man could not be king, he stepped down in favor of Bres. The new king was despised by the TUATHA people, who made a silver arm for Nuadhu so that he could return as their king. In English mythology he is known as Ludd; in Welsh mythology, as Nudd.

NUADHU AIRGEDLAMH A legendary king of the TUATHA DE DANAAN in Celtic mythology. Nuadhu led the Tuatha to victory in a great battle against the Fir Bholg, the first people of Ireland. But he lost an arm in the battle and had to give up the throne. The cruel new king, Bres, was so hated that Nuadhu was recalled by his people. Bres fled and raised an army against Nuadhu who, with the help of LUGH, led the Tuatha to a famous victory.

■

PERUNU The Slavic creator god and god of thunder and lightning. His worshipers prayed to him for rain by dancing in a circle around a virgin girl, who whirled around dressed only in flowers. The sweet smell and moisture of the flowers was thought to help persuade the rain to fall.

■

ROD The fertility god of the eastern Slavs and head of a cult that included the Rozhanitsy, the mother-daughter goddesses of fertility. (*See also* SVANTOVIT.)

RUSALKA Water spirits in Slavic mythology, believed to be the souls of drowned maidens. Like the Sirens of Greek mythology, they lure men to a watery grave with their singing. Similar spirits among the southern Slavs are the Vila, believed to be the souls of maidens who died before baptism or marriage.

■

SAULE The Baltic Sun goddess who scorches through the air in a chariot with copper wheels pulled by fiery horses that never tire. The Sun is believed to be a jug or ladle, and the sunshine to be a golden liquid pouring from it. Sacred to Saule are the zaltys, green snakes representing fertility. The death of a zaltys causes her to weep, and the red berries on the hillsides are said to be her tears.

■

SVANTOVIT The Slavic god of war. He has four heads, symbolizing his great power, and holds a bull-horn cup. Each year his worshipers would fill the horn with wine and later check the level to predict the harvest. The fuller the horn, the better the harvest. His temples each held a white horse sacred to the god, which was used to predict the outcome of war. Eastern Slavs associated Svantovit with ROD.

■

SVAROG The supreme Slavic god. He has two sons, Dazhbog (the Sun god) and SVAROZHICH (the god of fire).

■

SVAROZHICH The Slavic god of fire, especially the fire used to dry grain after the harvest. He could foretell the future, and humans were sacrificed to him.

■

TIWAZ The god of the sky and "god and ruler of all" in Germanic mythology. He is also a god of war and can bind people or set them free by using battle spells.

TUATHA DE DANAAN   The gods and people descended from the Celtic goddess DANAAN. The Tuatha were banished from Heaven because they had learned the knowledge of magic. They decided to live in Ireland, and after two great battles, first drove out the Fir Bholg, the original settlers, and then destroyed the evil Formorii. The Tuatha dominated Ireland until, in time, they too were defeated and driven into the mountains by the Sons of Mil. The most famous Tuatha kings were LUGH and NUADHU AIRGEDLAMH.

■

WAYLAND (WELAND) THE SMITH   The king of the elves in Anglo-Saxon and Germanic mythology. He was a renowned metalsmith of outstanding skill. He was captured by Nidud, the evil king of the Swedes, who forced the smith to work for him and cruelly made him lame. Wayland took dreadful revenge by killing Nidud's sons. He forged their skulls into silver-studded goblets and made jewelry from their eyes and teeth, before flying away with wings he had built himself.

WEREWOLVES AND VAMPIRES   Evil-spirited creatures, especially in Eastern European mythology. Werewolves are born with a red or saber-shaped birthmark, or with wolflike tufts of hair. They are believed to possess magic powers that allow them to see into the future and to turn into animals, especially the fierce forest wolf.

Vampires are the godless dead. They remain undecayed in their coffins and rise at night to suck the blood of those who sleep, often their own relatives.

■

WODAN   The god of the Underworld, poetry, and battle in Germanic mythology. He brings good fortune in war, but is really a sinister god who condemns his followers to defeat and death. Wodan is usually portrayed as a warrior on horseback, or as a wolf or raven—scavengers of the battlefield. In Anglo-Saxon mythology, he is known as Woden.

■

YARILO   The Slavic god of fertility and physical love. He is pictured dressed in white and crowned with wild flowers, holding a wheatsheaf in his arms.

▼ *Having killed King Nidud's sons and made their skulls into goblets, WAYLAND built wings from swan's feathers and flew to Nidud's palace. There he revealed the dreadful truth to the horrified court, before making his escape.*

41

· THE NORSE ·

From about A.D. 200 to 500, the Nordic people of northern and central Europe spread beyond their homelands into southern Sweden and Norway. Later, from the 700s, the Norsemen (as they had become known) left Scandinavia to spread west and east in search of new lands. The Norse were also called Vikings from around A.D. 700 to 1000. This name means something like "sudden raider."

The Norse settled in parts of the British Isles, Iceland, and Greenland, and east into Russia. At first, people shared common stories of the gods throughout all these areas. But as the new beliefs of Christianity were accepted, the myths died out. Most of the Norse myths that survive come to us from Scandinavia, which converted to Christianity around A.D. 1000, hundreds of years later than England and central Europe.

▲ *A Swedish tapestry from about A.D. 1100 shows the gods* ODIN, THOR, *and* FREY *on the right. These three were the main gods worshiped in Sweden before people converted to Christianity.*

Sources of the myths

The Norse passed their myths on through the oral tradition. Our knowledge of their beliefs comes mainly from literature written in the Middle Ages, especially in Iceland. The main sources are the *Elder Edda* and the *Prose Edda*.

▼ *The Vikings were fearless warriors both on sea and land, and the heroes in their myths were equally ready to face great danger.*

Early Norse beliefs stretch back at least as far as the Scandinavian Bronze Age (roughly from 1500 B.C. to 600 B.C.). Ancient rock carvings show a tall man with a spear, and other findings indicate that people also believed in an Earth goddess.

The *Elder Edda* contains poems about the myths by different poets. The *Prose Edda* was written by the 13th-century Icelandic chieftain, scholar, and poet Snorri Sturluson. He retells the Norse creation myths and the amazing deeds of their gods and goddesses, giants, dwarfs, elves, and heroes.

The Norse were a people used to hard weather, frequent war, and a rough life. To them the idea of struggle between gods and monsters came naturally. So, too, did a strong desire to explain the creation of the world and its structure.

The Norse creation

Before the world was made, there was only Ginnungagap, or "the Yawning." It lay between MUSPELL, a land of fire, and NIFLHEIM, a land of ice. As the ice and fire came together, they combined to make the giant, YMIR, and the cow, AUDUMLA. Other frost giants grew from Ymir's body. As Audumla licked the salty ice blocks with her rough tongue, the figure of Buri emerged. In time he had a son, Bor, who in his turn was father of ODIN, Vili, and Ve. These became the first gods.

When Odin and his brothers grew to adulthood, they killed Ymir and used parts of his body to make the world. His blood became the seas, his bones were made into mountains, and his flesh became the Earth itself. The Moon, Sun, and stars were made from sparks the gods took from Muspell.

Ymir's skull was used to make the sky. Four dwarfs grew from maggots on the giant's body. They were given the names North, South, East, and West, and each stood at a corner of the sky to hold it up.

Odin, Vili, and Ve then set about putting their new world in order. They made ASK AND EMBLA, the first people, from branches of the ash and the elm that they found by the sea. And they built ASGARD, the home of the gods.

▲ *The roots of* YGGDRASIL *lie in the Underworld. Its trunk is in Asgard, the home of the gods, and its branches reach to the heavens.*

The Norse believed the world was made up of several lands, or realms. The Earth, or MIDGARD, was one realm. An early Norse legend describes nine worlds that are placed one above the other within a World Tree, called YGGDRASIL. But in later Norse mythology, the tree crosses the various realms.

◄ *A memorial stone from Gotland in Sweden shows Odin being welcomed to his hall, Valhalla, by a Valkyrie maiden. Those warriors who died gloriously in battle were taken to Valhalla to live with Odin.*

◄ Thor's arch enemy is Jormungand, the World Serpent. Out fishing with the giant Hymir, Thor baited his line with an ox head and caught the serpent. There was a terrible struggle before the terrified Hymir cut Thor's line and let Jormungand escape.

Mortals live in Midgard, or Earth, which is seen as a circle of land with ocean all around. In the ocean depths, its body coiled right around the Earth, lives Jormungand, the terrible World Serpent.

Of the two races of gods, the AESIR live in Asgard and the Vanir in a realm called Vanaheim, beneath the Earth. Other worlds include those of the elves and the dwarfs, and of the Powers of Fate.

These worlds were linked by various routes. The most well known was BIFROST, the rainbow bridge between Asgard and Midgard. There were other routes that connected Asgard to Niflheim and to Jotunheim.

Yggdrasil has three roots. One reaches into Niflheim, the Underworld; another grows to Asgard. The third stretches to Jotunheim, land of the giants.

A serpent called NIDHOGG sits at the base of Yggdrasil and gnaws at its roots. An eagle sits in the top branches, and a squirrel runs up and down the tree carrying insults from eagle to serpent and back. A spring, the source of wisdom, bubbles from Yggdrasil's roots. A deer nibbles on its branches and a goat grazes nearby. From the deer's antlers flow the world's rivers, and from the goat comes mead to quench the thirst of Odin's warriors.

THOR, the god of thunder, was especially popular. Many people wore small copies of his symbol, the hammer, around their necks. At weddings, a hammer was laid in the bride's lap. A hammer was also sometimes carved on gravestones.

◀ This small bronze figure of a woman from Jutland in Denmark is believed to represent FREYA, the Norse goddess of fertility.

Menace of the giants

The Norse believed that both the gods and ordinary human beings were under constant threat from the giants. The giants envied the gods' great treasures, desired the goddess FREYA, and in their bitterness threatened to destroy the world, returning it to chaos.

To help the gods against the menace of the giants, warriors who had fallen in battle were taken to the hall of VALHALLA by Odin. There they fought, feasted, and waited for RAGNAROK, the final battle, when their help would be sorely needed.

▶ At RAGNAROK, the gods will battle with the giants. Odin will be killed by the wolf monster FENRIR.

The myth of Ragnarok explains how the world will end. In the time just before the battle, the rivalry and tension between the gods and the giants will increase. There will be constant war and anarchy on Earth. FENRIR will swallow the Sun and Moon. The stars will fall and the mountains crumble.

Ragnarok itself begins when the god LOKI breaks his bounds and, with the help of the fire giant SURT, leads the giants in an attack on Asgard. In the end both the giants and the gods are killed, and the Earth is set on fire by Surt. Only VIDAR, Magni, and the human couple LIF AND LIFRATHSIR will survive. They will inherit Asgard and a new green Earth—the ultimate expression of Norse belief that there is a better world to come.

To ensure good harvests and victory in battle, the Vikings made sacrifices to the gods at major festivals: Vetrarblot, held in October, Jolablot in January and Sigrblot in April. There was much feasting and drinking during the festivals.

The wall protecting ASGARD was pulled down in a war with the VANIR. A giant offered to rebuild the wall if FREYA agreed to marry him. The gods accepted, provided that the work was done in one winter. The task was virtually impossible, but the giant's mighty horse, Svadilfari, hauled the huge stones to the wall. Worried that Freya would have to marry the giant, the gods had LOKI pretend to be a mare and lure Svadilfari away. The work was never finished.

AEGIR   The god of the sea. He has nine daughters, said to be the maidens who move the waves. He is sometimes said to carry a spear, but more often he and his wife Ran are armed with a net to catch sailors, who are taken to the banqueting hall in Aegir's underwater kingdom.

■

AESIR AND VANIR   The names of the main groups of Norse gods and goddesses. At first the two fought each other, but in the end they called a truce so that they could unite against the giants. As a sign of peace, the Vanir leaders NJORD, FREYA, and FREY went to live among the Aesir. The Vanir are fertility gods and live in Vanaheim; the more important Aesir are the warrior gods led by ODIN, and who live in ASGARD.

■

ALFAR   The elves, magical creatures who are mostly harmless and often a help to farmers and fishermen, but can make mischief. They are associated with woods and the dead (especially burial mounds).

ANDVARI   A dwarf who owned a magic ring that could make gold. The ring and other treasure was stolen by LOKI to repay the king of the dwarfs for the loss of his son Otter, whom Loki had killed. Angered by the theft, Andvari put a curse on the ring and its treasure.

■

ANGRBODA   The giantess with whom LOKI fathered the three monsters, FENRIR, HEL, and Jormungand, the World Serpent.

■

ASGARD   Home of the AESIR. It is a great fortress, surrounded by a wall and connected to MIDGARD (Earth) by BIFROST, the rainbow bridge. Asgard includes VALHALLA, the Great Hall of ODIN; the halls of the other gods; and YGGDRASIL, the World Tree.

■

ASK AND EMBLA   The first man, created by the gods from an ash tree, and the first woman, created from an elm tree, on the seashore of MIDGARD (Earth).

▼ BALDER *was the best loved of all the gods, and after his tragic death they gave him a hero's farewell. His wife Nanna died of grief and was burned with him on his funeral pyre.*

◄ *The* DVERGAR, *or dwarfs, were renowned for their skill in working with gold, silver, and gems. Among the precious gifts they gave the gods are* ODIN's *gold ring* DRAUPNIR, THOR's *hammer Mjollnir, a boar with golden bristles, the magic chain, Gleipnir, which was used to bind the wolf monster* FENRIR, *as well as various magic rings, swords, and necklaces.*

AUDUMLA   A cow that existed in the great emptiness between MUSPELL and NIFLHEIM before the world began. She was created from drops of melted frost and lived by licking the salty, melting ice. Her continual licking gradually revealed Buri, father of Bor, who was in turn father of ODIN and his brothers.

■

BALDER   One of the AESIR, a son of ODIN and FRIGG, and husband of Nanna. He was the Sun god and stood for goodness, happiness, beauty, and wisdom. He could only be harmed by mistletoe and was killed by accident when HODER threw a dart of mistletoe at him.

■

BIFROST   The rainbow bridge linking MIDGARD (Earth) to ASGARD (Heaven). It is the only way into Asgard and is guarded by HEIMDALL, the "white god."

■

BRAGI   The god of poetry and knowledge. He is a son of ODIN and FRIGG and the husband of IDUNN. At ASGARD, Bragi welcomes slain warriors to VALHALLA and sings songs of the warrior heroes to them.

BRYNHILD   The leader of the VALKYRIES and the beautiful daughter of ODIN. She loved SIGURD, who had rescued her from a ring of fire. But Sigurd married Gudrun, whose mother had given him a magic potion that made him forget his love for Brynhild. Brynhild was heartbroken. When Sigurd rescued her from the ring of fire again, this time disguised as Gudrun's brother Gunnar, she married Gunnar believing him to be her savior. But she never forgave Sigurd, and out of jealousy arranged his murder. She was so overcome with remorse after this that she threw herself on Sigurd's funeral pyre.

■

DRAUPNIR   The golden ring of ODIN. It was forged by dwarfs and from it came all other rings. Every ninth night, eight more rings would drop from it. Odin laid Draupnir on BALDER's funeral pyre as a last gift. But when Balder's brother HERMOD was sent to the land of the dead to try to win his release, Balder gave Hermod the ring to take back to ASGARD.

■

DVERGAR (DWARFS)   Short, stocky, gray-bearded men created by the gods. They live in mountains and caves, and are renowned as skilled artisans, especially in working gold, silver, and gems. They are generally kind, but humans who steal their treasure usually meet with disaster.

In the 1800s, the German composer Richard Wagner set the story of BRYNHILD and SIGURD to music in his magnificent opera cycle *Der Ring des Nibelungen*, known in English as *The Ring Cycle*. In the operas, Brynhild is called Brunhild and Sigurd is known as Siegfried. This is because Wagner used Germanic, rather than Nordic, names.

▲ HEIMDALL *is the perfect watchman since he can see for vast distances and can hear the sound of wool growing on a sheep.*

F REY is the owner of Skidbladnir, a magic ship built by the dwarfs, which always has the wind in its favor. The ship is big enough to carry all the gods, yet it can be folded up so small that it fits into a pocket.

FAFNIR A man who turned into a dragon to guard the treasure he had taken from his father. But the treasure had once belonged to ANDVARI, who had put a curse upon it. Fafnir was killed by SIGURD, who inherited both the treasure and the curse.

■

FENRIR A wolf monster and the son of LOKI and the giantess ANGRBODA. When Fenrir roared, his lower jaw scraped the Earth and his snout lifted up to Heaven. He became so fierce that the gods decided he must be tied up. Only TYR was able to do this, using the magic chain, Gleipnir. Fenrir will break free at RAGNAROK, devour ODIN, and then be killed by VIDAR.

■

FREY The god of peace and fertility, son of NJORD and Skadi, and twin brother of· FREYA. He fell in love with GERD, a giantess of great beauty. Unable to leave ASGARD, he sent his servant, SKIRNIR, to Jotunheim, the home of the giants, to woo Gerd on his behalf. Frey gave Skirnir his magic sword (which always slew its opponent) as a reward. The servant persuaded Gerd to return with him to Asgard, where she and Frey were married. Frey will be killed by the fire giant SURT at the battle of RAGNAROK.

FREYA The goddess of fertility and love, daughter of NJORD and Skadi, and twin sister of FREY. She is the most beautiful of all the goddesses and is desired by many gods and men. Freya is also the goddess of battle and death, and has the right to choose half of all men slain in battle. She takes her fallen heroes to her great feasting hall of Folkvangar. The other half go to VALHALLA, where they feast with ODIN.

■

FRIGG The goddess of fertility and the home. She is the wife of ODIN, mother of BALDER, and queen of ASGARD. When Balder dreamed that he would soon be killed, Frigg was sent by the gods to make all living things promise not to harm him. All promised except the mistletoe, which Frigg failed to ask because it seemed so harmless. Then the blind god HODER was tricked by LOKI into throwing a shaft of mistletoe at Balder. It pierced Balder's heart and he fell down dead.

■

GARM The fearsome dog chained at the entrance to NIFLHEIM, where it guards the land of the dead. At the final battle of RAGNAROK, Garm will break free and fight with TYR, and they will kill each other.

■

GERD A fair maiden who lives in the frozen land of the frost giants, or in some versions of the story, in the Underworld. When seen by FREY in ASGARD, he sends his servant SKIRNIR to woo her for him.

■

GOLDEN APPLES *see* IDUNN

■

HEIMDALL Known as the "white god," he protects ASGARD by guarding BIFROST, the rainbow bridge. He will sound a horn to warn the gods as the giants approach Asgard at the start of RAGNAROK, where he and LOKI will fight and slay each other.

HEL The gruesome goddess of the dead who lives in NIFLHEIM (a world of mist and darkness, also known as the Underworld). She is the daughter of LOKI and the giantess ANGRBODA. Hel is very beautiful above the waist, but is rotting away below.

HERMOD The swift messenger of the gods and a son of ODIN and FRIGG. After his brother BALDER had been killed, Hermod sped to NIFLHEIM and pleaded with HEL for Balder's return to ASGARD. Hel agreed to release Balder if every living thing would weep for him. All Hermod's efforts were undone when LOKI, disguised as a giantess, refused to weep. For this, Loki was punished.

HODER The blind god. LOKI persuaded him to join the other gods who were throwing objects at BALDER as a joke, after FRIGG had made all things agree not to harm him. But she failed to ask the mistletoe. Loki fashioned a dart from this and gave it to Hoder when it was his turn to throw. The dart pierced Balder's heart.

HRUNGNIR A giant who challenged ODIN to a horse race. By mistake the riders crossed into ASGARD, where giants had never been welcome. Even so, Hrungnir was offered drink, but the more he drank the ruder he became. THOR grew so angry that he challenged the giant to a duel. Hrungnir threw his whetstone at Thor, and Thor threw his hammer at Hrungnir. The weapons met in the air. The whetstone shattered, and Hrungnir was killed by Thor's hammer.

IDUNN The wife of BRAGI and the goddess who guards the Golden Apples of Youth that keep the gods immortal. The giant Thiazi, in the form of an eagle, captured Idunn and stole the apples, after LOKI had tricked her into leaving the safety of ASGARD. Without the apples the gods began to grow old. They threatened to kill Loki unless he stole them back.

JOTNAR (GIANTS) The legendary first race, who live in Jotunheim. The body of YMIR, the first giant, was used to create the Earth. The giants are the enemies of the gods and are destined to overcome them at RAGNAROK, the final battle.

▲ *The gods changed* LOKI *into a falcon so he could steal back the Golden Apples of Youth. Changing* IDUNN *into a nut, Loki flew off with her, chased by Thiazi in the form of an eagle. As Loki crossed back to* ASGARD, *the gods singed Thiazi's wings with fire and killed him when he fell from the sky.*

Famous giants include ANGRBODA, HRUNGNIR, Hymir (with whom Thor fished for the World Serpent), SURT, SUTTUNG, Thiazi (who stole the Golden Apples of Youth from the gods), Thrym (who stole Thor's hammer), and UTGARD-LOKI. AEGIR and his wife Ran are also sometimes said to be giants.

YGGDRASIL, the World Tree, is watered by three goddesses called the Norns. They decide the fate of both gods and humankind and are called Urd (Fate), Verdandi (Being), and Skuld (Necessity).

▼ MUSPELL *is the home of the fire giants. Chief among them is* SURT, *who will lead the giants against the gods at* RAGNAROK.

KVASIR   The wisest god. When the AESIR and the VANIR united in peace, they spat into a bowl to seal the truce. From the saliva, the gods created Kvasir. He was killed by two dwarfs, but his blood was caught in a cauldron and mixed with honey to create the mead of inspiration, poetry, and wisdom. The giant SUTTUNG took the mead from the dwarfs, but ODIN was able to steal it back.

■

LIF AND LIFRATHSIR   Lif (Life) is a man and Lifrathsir (Eager for Life) is a woman. They will survive the destruction of RAGNAROK by hiding in the World Tree and go on to found a new race of people.

■

LOKI   A trickster god known for his cunning and mischief-making. With the giantess ANGRBODA he fathered HEL, FENRIR, and Jormungand, the World Serpent. He traveled with THOR on many of his adventures. For his part in BALDER's death, the gods bound Loki to the Earth beneath a snake that drops its burning poison on his face. He will break free at RAGNAROK, and he and HEIMDALL will kill each other.

MIDGARD   The Earth, or world of humans, which lies midway between ASGARD and Jotunheim, the land of the frost giants. Midgard was created from the body of YMIR, the first giant, after he had been slain by ODIN and his brothers. It is joined to Asgard by the rainbow bridge BIFROST. YGGDRASIL, the World Tree, has the second of its three roots planted in Midgard.

■

MUSPELL   Before the world existed, Muspell (also known as Muspellheim) and NIFLHEIM were the only places. In between was an emptiness. Muspell is the realm of fire, and its heat helped in the creation of the world by melting the ice in the emptiness to form AUDUMLA and YMIR.

■

NIDHOGG   The evil dragon monster that lives in Nastrond (the shore of corpses) within the realm of NIFLHEIM. It tries to kill YGGDRASIL, the World Tree, by gnawing at its root and feeds on the bodies of the dead, especially of evildoers.

■

NIFLHEIM   A world of ice, mist, and darkness where the land of the dead is to be found. The deepest root of YGGDRASIL, the World Tree, is planted in Niflheim, where it is gnawed at by NIDHOGG, the dragon monster. Niflheim is ruled by HEL, and its entrance is guarded by GARM, the savage dog.   (*See also* MUSPELL.)

■

NJORD   A god of the sea and winds and the protector of sailors. He is the leader of the VANIR and father of FREY and FREYA. He brought peace between the two groups of gods by moving with his family to live among the AESIR. His wife is Skadi, a great huntress and daughter of the giant Thiazi. But they live apart since Njord cannot bear to be away from the sea, and Skadi is only happy in the forests.

ODIN   The chief of the gods, especially of the AESIR, and king of ASGARD. He is also known as the All-Father. Odin is god of battle and death, and can begin a war by throwing down his spear. With his brothers, Ve and Vili, he slew the giant YMIR to create MIDGARD (the Earth) and set the Sun and the Moon in motion. He gave life to ASK AND EMBLA, the first people. His wife is FRIGG, but she is not the mother of all of his children.

Odin is also god of wisdom or magic, inspiration, and prophesy. He gained his knowledge after going through many acts of self-sacrifice. He hanged himself from YGGDRASIL, the World Tree, to learn the secrets of the dead. He gave up an eye for a single drink from Mimir, the spring of knowledge in the land of the giants.

He rules over the hall of VALHALLA, where he welcomes half the warriors slain in battle (the other half go to FREYA). Odin is destined to die at RAGNAROK, when he will be eaten by the wolf monster FENRIR.

RAGNAROK   The final battle at the end of the present world, to be fought between the gods and the giants on the Plain of Vigrid. The only gods to survive are Magni, the son of THOR, and VIDAR, the son of ODIN.   (See page 45.)

REGIN   A brother of FAFNIR the dragon. Fafnir had murdered their father, Hreidmar, and stolen from him ANDVARI's treasure. Regin urged SIGURD to avenge the death by killing Fafnir, and to take the treasure the dragon guarded. Regin forged a sword so strong it could slice through an anvil and, armed with this weapon, Sigurd slew the dragon. But Regin's real plan was to kill Sigurd afterward and take the treasure for himself. Sigurd learned of the treachery and beheaded Regin.

▲ SIGURD *killed the dragon* FAFNIR *and captured his treasure. But the treasure carried a curse that brought ill fate to all who owned it, and in the end Sigurd himself was killed.*

SIGURD   A hero of immense strength, courage, and beauty. He was an orphan, brought up by the evil smith REGIN, who told him the sorry tale of ANDVARI's treasure and of the evil dragon FAFNIR that guarded it. At Regin's urging, Sigurd killed Fafnir. The dragon's blood, which dripped from Sigurd's hand, had magic powers. When he licked his fingers clean, Sigurd found that he could understand the speech of birds, who warned him that Regin intended treachery. Sigurd beheaded Regin and took the treasure.

SIGYN   The faithful wife of LOKI. Loki was bound to the Earth beneath a poisonous snake for his part in the slaying of BALDER. Sigyn catches the snake's venom in a bowl. Whenever she has to empty the bowl, the burning poison drops on Loki's face. So great is his agony that his struggles cause the Earth to tremble.

▼ ODIN *owns the eight-legged horse Sleipnir, which can gallop over land, sea, and air.*

▲ The magic chain that bound FENRIR was made from the sinew of a bear, the spit of a bird, the sound of a cat's step, the breath of a fish, the root of a mountain, and the beard of a woman. As the wolf monster struggled to free itself, all the gods laughed, except TYR, whose hand was in Fenrir's mouth.

Originally, the first race of giants included the trolls. These huge, bad-tempered creatures were special foes of THOR. Later, the trolls became more like dwarfs. They lived in the mountains and became skilled at crafts.

SKIRNIR
The servant of FREY who helped to woo the beautiful giantess GERD, and win her as his master's bride.

■

SURT   The chief fire giant of MUSPELL. At RAGNAROK he will ride at the head of his army and cross into ASGARD, over the rainbow bridge BIFROST, which will shatter beneath the weight. He will join forces with the frost giants on the Plain of Vigrid and in the battle all giants will be slain except Surt, who will destroy both Asgard and the Earth with a storm of fire.

■

SUTTUNG   A giant whose parents were killed by the two dwarfs who had slain KVASIR. The dwarfs gave Suttung the mead of wisdom to save their lives, after he had put them on a rock in the sea and threatened to leave them there to drown. ODIN stole the mead back by boring a hole into the deep mountain cavern where Suttung kept it safe. Taking the form of a snake, Odin wriggled through the hole and reached the cavern. He stored the mead in his mouth and escaped back to ASGARD in the shape of an eagle.

THOR   The mighty god of thunder and of the Sun, and one of the chief gods of the AESIR. He is the eldest son of ODIN and his mother is said to be the Earth. Thor is a good friend to humankind and the sworn enemy of the JOTNAR (giants).

His most famous possession is his hammer, called Mjollnir, made by dwarfs. One blow from the hammer means instant death, and it always returns to Thor of its own will. He also has a magic belt, which doubles his strength, and iron gloves with which he can handle any weapon. As god of the sky he scorches through the air in a chariot pulled by giant goats. Thunder booms from his hammer and lightning crashes from the wheels of his chariot.

■

THRYM   A frost giant who hid THOR's magic hammer, Mjollnir. Thor's friend LOKI changed into a falcon and searched for the hammer and discovered that Thrym had been the thief. Thrym refused to return it unless he could wed the goddess FREYA. The marriage was agreed, but it was Thor who went to Jotunheim, the home of the frost giants, disguised as Freya. When the hammer was brought out at the ceremony, Thor seized it and slew Thrym and all the wedding guests.

■

TYR   A god of war, the patron of athletes, and a son of ODIN and FRIGG. When the gods decided to tie up the wolf monster FENRIR, they asked the dwarfs to forge a magic chain strong enough to hold it. Fenrir was so ferocious that it could only be bound if the gods first tricked it into believing that they would afterward set it free. Fenrir did not trust the gods, so Tyr put his hand in the wolf's mouth as an act of good faith. When Fenrir was bound and not set free, it bit off Tyr's hand. Tyr was thereafter known as the One Handed.

UTGARD-LOKI The giant ruler of Utgard, a land beyond ASGARD. When THOR, LOKI, and a man, Thialfi, journeyed to this realm, Utgard-Loki set them several tasks.

Loki was matched against the giant Logi in an eating race. Thialfi was pitted against another giant, Hugi, in a foot race. Thor was given a huge horn to drink from, a large cat to lift, and Utgard-Loki's old foster mother to wrestle. All three friends failed miserably and were humiliated. When Utgard-Loki accompanied them back to the entrance of Utgard he told them the truth. Logi is Fire and consumes all things. Hugi is Thought and swifter than any man. The horn offered to Thor had its end in a deep ocean; the cat is Jormungand, the World Serpent; and Utgard-Loki's foster mother is Old Age, whom no one can overcome.

VALHALLA The hall of warriors slain in battle; its walls were made of shields and its roof of swords.

VALKYRIES Beautiful warrior maidens led by their chief, BRYNHILD. They are the attendants and messengers of ODIN at the hall of VALHALLA in ASGARD. They choose who will be slain in battle and ride through the sky on horses to fetch Odin's share of the fallen heroes.

VANIR *see* **AESIR AND VANIR**

VIDAR A strong, silent god and son of ODIN. At RAGNAROK, which he will survive, he will avenge the death of his father by slaying the wolf monster FENRIR.

YMIR The first giant, also known as Aurgelmir, whose body made MIDGARD. Ymir was slain by the three gods ODIN, Vili, and Ve. His flesh formed the Earth; his bones became the mountains; his teeth became the rocks and stones; his blood filled the rivers and seas; and his brains were tossed in the air to make the clouds.

YGGDRASIL The World Tree. Of its three roots, one reaches to ASGARD, one descends to NIFLHEIM, and the third goes to Jotunheim, land of the giants. (See page 43.)

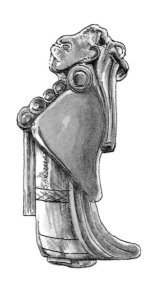

▼ *This silver pendant, made in Lapland about A.D. 500, may have been intended to represent a* VALKYRIE.

▼ *The* VALKYRIES, *wearing battle dress, carry warriors killed in battle to the hall of* VALHALLA.

·AFRICA·

Africa is an enormous continent. Three times the size of Europe, it is the second largest continent in the world and there are nearly a thousand languages spoken there. Some are widely used, while others are known by only a few hundred people. This means that there are a great number of peoples and many different mythologies.

South of the Sahara, Africa is often divided into western, central, eastern, and southern regions; but there is no hard and fast line between these zones. African mythology has a great many themes that are similar over these areas as a whole, but with different names from region to region. For example, a World Serpent appears in Benin as Dan Ayido Hwedo; a similar figure in Zaire is known as Nkongolo. Other examples of widespread themes are explanations for the origin of death, and stories about the origins and early migrations of peoples.

Until the last century, nearly all of Africa had no written language and depended on oral records in which the names of kings or other historical events were preserved in the memory of the older people in the community. Arabic writing was used in the Saharan region of West Africa from about A.D. 1100, but it was not used to write down myths. Until the 1800s and later when European travelers, missionaries, and historians came to write down surviving traditions and myths, hardly any African myths were known outside their country of origin.

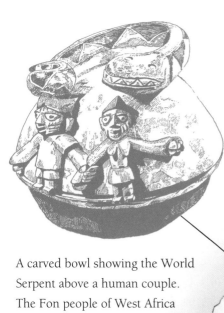

A carved bowl showing the World Serpent above a human couple. The Fon people of West Africa believe that a serpent brought life to the Earth and now helps support it with his body.

MA

GHANA

Niger River

ATLANTIC OCEAN

Mende
Ashanti

▼ *The ruins of Great Zimbabwe, a walled city which was built between* A.D. *1000 and* A.D. *1400. The massive granite walls may have enclosed sacred buildings as well as a royal palace.*

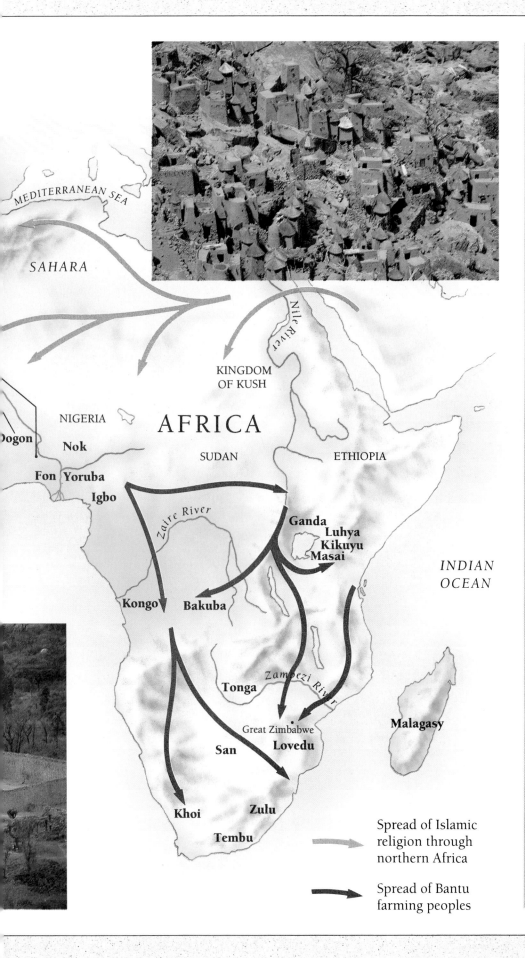

The houses of a Dogon village cling to the terraced slopes of the Bandiagara Cliffs in Mali. The thatch-topped buildings are for grain storage.

MEDITERRANEAN SEA

SAHARA

Nile River

KINGDOM OF KUSH

NIGERIA

AFRICA

Dogon

Nok

SUDAN

ETHIOPIA

Fon Yoruba

Igbo

Zaire River

Ganda
Luhya
Kikuyu
Masai

INDIAN OCEAN

Kongo Bakuba

Tonga

Zambezi River

Great Zimbabwe

Malagasy

San Lovedu

Khoi Zulu

Tembu

Spread of Islamic religion through northern Africa

Spread of Bantu farming peoples

TIME LINE

B.C.

c. 2500 Fertile grasslands in the Sahara begin to dry out

c. 750 The powerful ancient kingdom of Kush, based in Sudan, conquers Egypt

c. 600 Bantu farming peoples begin to migrate from their homelands in West Africa toward southern Africa

c. 430 The Greek historian Herodotus reports that the people of Kush worship the Greek gods Zeus and Dionysus

c. 400 Nok culture flourishes in Nigeria

A.D.

c. 350 Christianity reaches Ethiopia

c. 700 Most of North Africa is now controlled by Arabs and has been converted to the Islamic religion

700-1200 Kingdom of Ghana grows rich on trade

1235 Kingdom of Mali established

c. 1300 Great Zimbabwe emerges as center of major trading empire

c. 1510 First African slaves taken to North America

55

·AFRICA·

All over Africa, people believe in a supreme being. This deity has more than 200 main names in many different languages. The people of Mali know this god as AMMA, while the Tembu people of South Africa speak of UMDALI. The supreme god is normally also the creator, but is simply too remote to be concerned with human affairs. This is the case almost everywhere in Africa south of the Sahara that has not converted to Islam or Christianity.

When people offer prayers or worship, it is usually to lesser gods or spirits, each of whom has a distinct function. Some of these may be real or mythical ancestors of the community who have become larger than life in the stories told about them. TSUI'GOAB of Namibia may be such a figure.

If something goes badly wrong, it is often seen as a sign that a community ancestor is angry and has to be appeased.

In many African creation myths, people once lived with the supreme god until they did something annoying. Then they were banished to Earth. According to a Malagasy myth, the supreme god sent his son to Earth on a mission. But it was so hot that the son fled down a hole to escape the heat. When the son did not return, his father sent human beings to search for him. The son could not be found, and messengers were sent back to Heaven for advice. These did not return and are said to be the dead.

◄ *According to a Masai myth, the supreme god took the first cattle away from the pygmy Dorobo and gave them to the Masai, sending them to Earth via a leather thong. Dorobo broke the thong with an arrow, severing the link between Heaven and Earth.*

▲ In a Krachi myth, death was a giant clothed in long hair. People set fire to his hair while he slept and killed him. But a curious boy put the powder of life in one of the giant's eyes: now each time the eye blinks, someone dies.

The lands of the spirits

In all parts of Africa, people believe that the dead continue to exist as spirits. Some people, such as the Zulu, believe that the spirits live in the sky, while others, such as the Igbo of Nigeria, believe that they live in an underground kingdom.

The Kongo people of western Zaire say that the universe is divided into two parts: the living dwell in the upper world, and the dead in the Underworld. Although the two worlds are similar (each has water, hills, and villages) the Underworld faces downward.

Other myths set out to explain mysteries of life and nature, such as why death came to the world. In many African myths, there was no death at first: it came into the world because someone broke the rules, or was lazy or ungrateful. Sometimes, it is an animal that brings death: a myth from Sudan blames the hyena and weaverbird.

▲ Antique stone figures, called nomoli, are dug up by the Mende people of Sierra Leone, who believe that they are rice gods who will protect their crops.

A myth told by the Luhya of Kenya explains night and day. The supreme god, Wele, first made Heaven and then made the Sun and Moon, so that they could help him with the rest of the universe.

Unfortunately, the two began to fight. The Moon knocked the Sun out of the sky; the Sun covered the Moon with mud. In the end, Wele was forced to decide that the two should never appear in the sky together: now the Sun shines during the day and the Moon at night.

In African mythology, as elsewhere in the world, people often obtain fire by stealing. In a myth of the Fang people, men stole fire from the supreme god, whose mother died as a result. After this, the god decided that all people shall also die.

The forces of nature

In Africa, the forces of nature sometimes seem huge and fearsome. That is why thunder and lightning may be linked with a powerful figure who can control them, such as the Yoruba storm god SHANGO.

Drought can be a terrible disaster, bringing failed crops and dying livestock. So someone like MODJADJI, the Lovedu rain queen, may be needed to control rainfall.

Rain is the subject of myths all over Africa. In Kenya, the Luhya group of peoples have a story of how an old woman found out how to control rain. But thunder and lightning came at the same time, which made people so afraid that they drove her away.

The old woman went to live with a man, and told him how to make rain fall. He made use of this knowledge and began to ask for payment for his work.

According to a myth told by the Kikuyu people of Kenya, the rainbow in the sky is the reflection of the dreadful rainbow monster. This creature lives underwater, but comes out under cover of night to eat animals and, sometimes, people.

▼ A myth about KINTU, the ancestor of the Ganda of Uganda, tells how he fooled the king of Heaven into believing that he had eaten enough food to feed 100 people by dropping most of it into a hole in the floor.

Danger from natural forces, such as flood, crop failure, sickness among people or livestock, or plagues of locusts, may be turned aside by the right offerings to the local spirit. Nothing is left to chance in African beliefs.

Stories about ancestor heroes or gods of the community are popular. These myths may be told to provide a good example for people to follow, or to foster a sense of pride in a people's

history. Former kings or chiefs performed amazing feats of strength or cunning, and might turn into lesser gods. Shango, who was once a king in Nigeria, was one such figure. Another was KINTU of Uganda, who passed five "impossible" tests to win the king of Heaven's daughter.

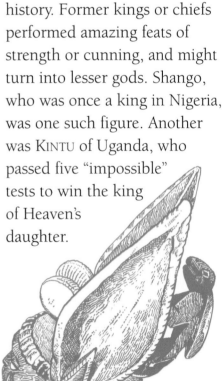

▶ HARE often appears in African art, such as on this mask with enormous hare's ears from the Yoruba of Nigeria.

In western Africa, it is said that the Sun and the Moon are man and wife. The couple always argue, and the Sun chases and tries to eat the Moon. When there is a lunar eclipse, people shout and beat their drums to make the Sun let go of the Moon.

Tricksters

Trickster figures—mischievous characters who may be human, animal, or both, and hinder or help humans—are popular in Africa. One of the best known is ESHU. To the Yoruba people of Nigeria, he causes all the arguments between human beings. Whenever there is change he is there, and he decides what part chance shall play in an individual's life.

Eshu is the reason that the supreme god withdrew from the world in the first place, but because he is able to speak every language, he now acts as the messenger from the gods to humans and takes the people's offerings to the gods. Eshu is known as Legba by the Fon people of Benin.

▶ *Spider avenged himself on Lion by tricking him into getting tied up in knots and secured to a large tree. He then ate Lion's food without sharing it.*

As in European folklore, in African mythology animals often behave and talk just like people. They too appear in trickster myths. The hero of these stories is usually a small animal that manages to get the better of a larger, stronger one.

TORTOISE is a popular trickster. So too is Spider, who is known as ANANSE by the Ashanti, and HARE. Many of the stories about Brer Rabbit, who is a trickster in American folklore, are really stories about Hare that crossed to North America with African slaves.

In some African myths, animals help with the creation of the world or shape human civilization. According to the San people of southwest Africa, the praying mantis invented language and stole fire from the ostrich to give to people.

Many Africans believe that almost every object in nature has its own spirit. As well as animals and humans, this includes mountains, rivers, and trees. In Kenya, whole families of spirits are said to live in the baobab tree.

Some spirits are said to be evil, and there is a widespread belief in magic. Stories are told about men or women who may be witches and fly through the air at night to suck the life out of other people in the village. Only a "witch doctor" has the knowledge needed to drive these evil spirits away.

▲ All the creatures found on Earth were stolen from AMMA by the ancestors of the Dogon people. A male and female of each animal in Heaven and a sample of every plant were collected and placed in a giant pyramid, which slid down to Earth on a rainbow. Fire was brought to Earth at the same time by a thread that was attached to the pyramid at one end and to an arrow thrust into the Sun at the other.

AMMA The supreme god of the Dogon people of Mali, West Africa. He made the Sun, the Moon, and the stars. Amma became lonely and mated with the Earth. Divine twins were born, and they stood for water and light, the life force of the world. Then Amma created the first man and woman, who had four more pairs of twins, the ancestors of the Dogon people. Twins are a common theme in African mythology, especially in West Africa.

■

ANANSE The Ashanti of Ghana tell many stories of Ananse, a spider who behaves like a man. One story tells how he captured a fairy called Mmoatia by covering a doll with sticky rubber.

■

DAN AYIDO HWEDO A giant python and the first creation of Mawa, the supreme god of the Fon people of West Africa. Together Mawa and Dan Ayido Hwedo made the Earth, but the supreme god was worried that the Earth might sink and drown under the weight of the mountains, trees, and big animals. So he asked the great python to encircle the Earth and to hold it tight by gripping its tail in its mouth. To the Fon people, and others throughout the world, a snake that has shed its skin seems to be newborn, and when shown coiled with its tail in its mouth represents immortality or eternity.

▶ HARE once tricked the elephant and the hippo into a tug-of-war with one another by pretending to each that he was at the other end of the rope.

ESHU The mischievous messenger of the gods among the Yoruba of southern Nigeria. He is always seen with strings of cowrie shells with which he tells the future. Eshu can be unpredictable, violent, and a spreader of false rumors. Only OLODUMARE has the power to control him.

■

HARE A trickster figure found in stories in most parts of Africa. One southern African story tells how Hare lost humans the chance of immortality. The Moon sent Hare to the first people with the message, "Just as the Moon dies and rises again so shall you." But Hare got the message wrong and told them, "Just as the Moon dies and perishes so shall you." When the Moon found out what Hare had said, she beat him on the nose with a stick, and since that day Hare's nose has been split.

■

KINTU The first man and the ancestor hero of the Ganda people of Uganda. Kintu fell in love with Nambi, the daughter of Gulu, the king of Heaven. Gulu did not approve of Kintu and set him five difficult tests. When Kintu succeeded in each, Gulu said the two could wed. They went to live on Earth, taking with them animals and fruit: some cows, a sheep, a goat, a hen, a banana, and a yam.

LEZA The supreme god of many peoples of central Africa. He is an ancient god, and when his eyes water with old age, the tears form rain. A story of the Tonga people tells how he once decided that the entire family of a young woman should die. The unhappy woman tried to find her way to Heaven to ask Leza why he was causing her such grief. She built a ladder to the sky, but the ladder crumbled as she climbed. She looked for the road leading to Heaven, but could not find it. When she asked people for directions, they told her that humankind was destined to suffer, and that she was no exception.

MODJADJI A rain queen among the Lovedu people of the Transvaal, South Africa. She is also known as Mujaji. The Lovedu call upon her in times of drought, when she uses secret charms and the help of her ancestors to make rain and keep the land in good health.

MOON The San of western Namibia link the rising and waning of the Moon with the coming of death to the world. In western Africa, there is a story that the Sun and the Moon invited water to visit them. Their house was flooded, so they had to move to a new home up in the sky.

NKULUNKULU The supreme god of the Zulu of southern Africa. He created the world and controls the rising and setting of the Sun and Moon, the wind and rain, lightning and thunder, floods and drought, and disease. He provides people with cattle and grain, but otherwise is a remote figure.

NYAME The supreme god of the Ashanti people of Ghana. Different aspects of Nyame rule the sky, the Earth, and the Underworld. Thunderbolts are called Nyame's Axes, and the Ashanti place stone axes in Nyame's Tree, a forked post by the house door, with offerings in a pot. He helps those in hardship or distress. Nyame also gave the Ashanti the sacred Golden Stool, which contains the soul of the Ashanti, and also their health and welfare. It is still in the royal palace at Kumasi.

ODUDUWA The first king of the Yoruba people in southern Nigeria. OLODUMARE delegated the task of creating the world to Orishanla, who was chief of the lesser gods and destined to be Olodumare's deputy on Earth. But Orishanla grew sleepy after drinking palm wine and did not finish the job. Oduduwa discovered him asleep and completed the work of creation himself. Oduduwa then took the place of Orishanla, becoming owner of the land and founder of the Yoruba people.

OGO One of the first beings created by AMMA, in Dogon mythology. Amma was very slow to create a female twin for Ogo, who grew impatient and forced himself upon Mother Earth. This caused chaos in the universe, and Amma punished Ogo by turning him into a lonely, destructive jackal. It is now the job of humankind to bring order back to the world through honoring the gods.

One of the tests set by Gulu for KINTU was to find his own cow, which Gulu had hidden among several herds of identical cows. This would have been an impossible task but for a bee that took pity on Kintu. It told him to get the herds to file past and to choose the animal with a bee buzzing around its horns—that would be Kintu's cow.

The Golden Stool given by NYAME to the Ashanti was brought down from the sky by a legendary magician called Anotochi. The stool is used on ceremonial occasions when it is carried under a magnificent umbrella. No one may sit upon the stool, though the king of the Ashanti pretends to do so as part of the ritual.

▼ A Yoruba priest throws palm nuts from one hand to the other before tossing them into a carved wooden bowl. From the patterns made by the nuts, the priest interprets messages from ORUNMILA, who is also known as Ifa, the Yoruba word for divining. This is known as the Ifa system of divination.

OGUN   The Yoruba god of iron and the eldest son of ODUDUWA. He is the patron of all those who use iron, such as hunters and blacksmiths. Ogun is both respected and feared; an oath sworn in his name, with the tongue touching a knife blade or other iron object, is completely binding.

OLODUMARE   The supreme god of the Yoruba. In the beginning only the sky and the sea existed. Olodumare created seven crowned princes, who became the first crowned kings of the Yoruba, and a pack of black matter, which became the Earth. His supremacy was once challenged by Olokun, the god of water and riches. The supreme god sent his messenger, the chameleon, to meet the challenge. Olokun tried to outdo Olodumare by putting on a series of increasingly splendid robes. Each time the chameleon matched them exactly, until at last Olokun, humiliated by a mere messenger, gave up the challenge.

ORUNMILA   The god of divination, which is the art of learning about the unknown future by using magical means. He was sent to Earth by OLODUMARE to teach people the civilized arts and medicine. Orunmila knows all the languages of the world, and is said to be an oracle. His messages are interpreted from the patterns made by palm nuts thrown by Yoruba priests.

OSANYIN   The god of the herbs and plants used in medicine and the ceremonies of the Yoruba people. He is closely linked with ORUNMILA, the god of divination, since diviners are consulted to find the cause of illness or bad luck. It is said that while Orunmila gave names to all the plants, it was Osanyin who knew the healing properties of each of them.

OSHOSSI   The god of hunters among the Yoruba of southern Nigeria. He is an important god who protects the hunters and makes sure that they come home with a good bag of game. As hunters spend a lot of time in the forest, they get to know where to find medicinal plants and good sites for a new village or farm. Since hunters often carry weapons, they play an important role as keepers of the peace.

SHANGO   The legendary third king of the Yoruba and the son of the god Oranyan. He was a fierce, fire-breathing ruler, but when challenged by his enemies, he fled into the forest. It is said that Shango rose to Heaven and became the god of thunder and lightning. Shango hates liars and thieves. It is a sign of his anger, and evidence of guilt, to be struck by lightning. Shango's emblem, the double ax, represents thunderbolts, and his devotees dance in his honor waving staffs with the double ax at the end.

TORTOISE Slow-moving Tortoise is the hero of some of the popular stories about small animals getting the better of larger ones. The most famous of these stories, also found elsewhere in the world, concerns a race between HARE and Tortoise. Tortoise won the contest with the help of his family, which he placed at intervals along the racetrack. No matter how fast Hare ran, Tortoise always appeared to be ahead of him.

TSUI'GOAB A rain god and hero of the Khoi people of southern Africa. He fought with Gaunab, who may have been death, and after a long struggle defeated him. As he was dying, Gaunab lashed out and hit Tsui'goab on the knee. Hence the hero's name, which means "wounded knee." Tsui'goab now lives in the sky, and people pray to him to send rain to water their crops and to provide drink for their flocks.

UMDALI The supreme god among the Tembu of southern Africa. In times of great trouble, such as drought or epidemic, people appeal to Umdali. First they spend a week avoiding all wrongdoing, since Umdali must be approached in a state of purity. Then they hold a special ceremony. Those taking part consume sacred corn and beer, and sing a prayer before offering Umdali gifts.

WOOT Sometimes called Woto, he is a magician and the father of the Bakuba people of Zaire. Woot was the elder of twins, born to an old couple after they received a visit from a stranger from the sky, who told them that he was the Lord.

YEMANJA A river goddess among the Yoruba. Her name means "the mother whose children are fishes." She is the daughter of Olokun, god of the sea, and the wife first of ORUNMILA, and then Olofin, a king of the Yoruba. She had ten children by different fathers, including the rainbow and the thunder god SHANGO.

▲ *A mask representing* WOOT *is worn during a special Bakuba ceremony. The mask is decorated with shells and beads and can only be worn by men of the royal family.*

As the patron of those who use iron, today OGUN looks after motorists, train drivers, and all mechanics.

·Mediterranean· Lands

The earliest Mediterranean civilizations grew up in the Near East and Egypt thousands of years ago. The peoples fought and traded with each other for centuries until, in the 300s B.C., Alexander the Great invaded and conquered Egypt and Persia. Alexander's conquests spread Greek culture over a huge area, and Greek became the official language throughout the Near East.

By the time of Christ, the whole of the Mediterranean region had been conquered by the Romans. They expected subjected peoples to worship Roman gods, but they also allowed local religious customs and mythologies to continue.

The constant contact between different cultures meant that mythological ideas were often shared throughout the region. For instance, some scholars believe that the Greeks adopted their creation myth from the Near East.

Differences in the myths reflect each area's own religious and social attitudes. For example, Greek myths were affected by political change. When Athens became a democracy during the 400s B.C., myths began to involve ordinary human beings. In comparison, the myths of the powerful monarchies of Egypt and the Near East concentrated on gods, kings, and queens.

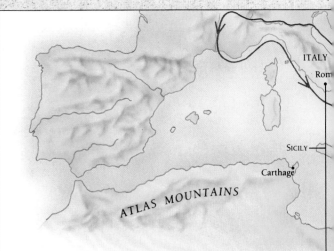

▲ The ancient Greek gods made their will known through the Oracle at the temple of Apollo. The ruins of the temple still stand at Delphi in Greece.

→ Route taken by Jason and the Argonauts

⟶ Route taken by Alexander the Great

Statue of a Roman lar (a household god)

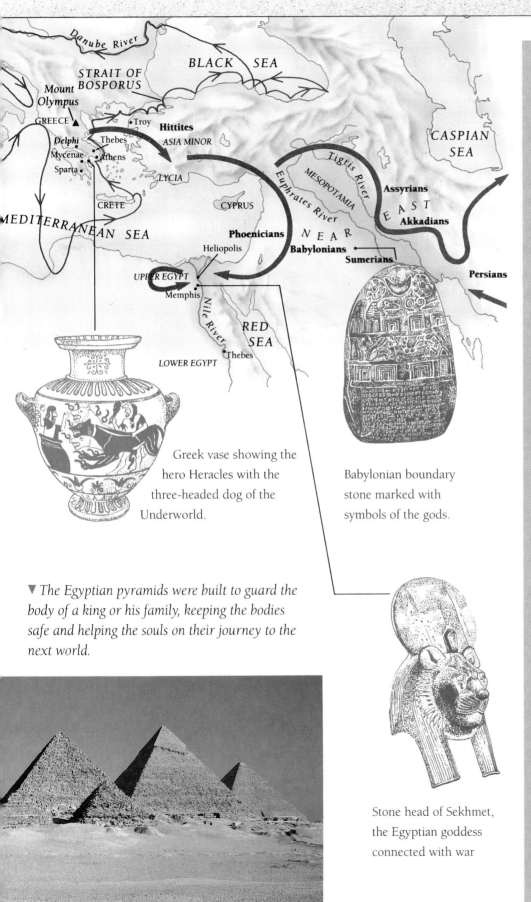

Greek vase showing the hero Heracles with the three-headed dog of the Underworld.

Babylonian boundary stone marked with symbols of the gods.

▼ *The Egyptian pyramids were built to guard the body of a king or his family, keeping the bodies safe and helping the souls on their journey to the next world.*

Stone head of Sekhmet, the Egyptian goddess connected with war

TIME LINE

B.C.

c. **3000** Upper and Lower Egypt unite under one ruler

2600–1850 Period of the Sumerian city-states

1925 Hittites conquer Babylon

1600–1100 Mycenaean civilization flourishes

c. **1550** New Kingdom begins: period of Egypt's greatest power

1116 Assyrians conquer Babylon

c. **1250** Trojan War begins

900–750 Rise of Greek city-states

753 City of Rome founded

669 Assyrians conquer Egypt

625–539 Period of the Neo-Babylonian empire

621 First laws written down in Athens

539–331 Persian empire dominates Mesopotamia

509 Kings expelled from Rome: Republic founded

479 Greece wins Persian wars

c. **332** Alexander the Great conquers the Persian empire

241 Rome becomes the dominant power in Italy

c. **146** Rome conquers Greece

31 Romans defeat Cleopatra, the last queen of Egypt

A.D.

235 Rome: 50 years of Barbarian invasion begin

380 Christianity becomes religion of Roman empire

· THE NEAR EAST ·

At the center of the ancient Near East was Mesopotamia, found in the valleys of the Tigris and Euphrates rivers. From around 3300 B.C., it was occupied by a succession of different states, which developed at the same time as ancient Egypt.

The first peoples to settle in Mesopotamia were the Akkadians and Sumerians. They built cities and developed organized religions based on a rich mythological tradition. They were followed by the Assyrians in the north and the Babylonians in the south. These new cultures kept the ancient myths. Neighboring civilizations, such as the Phoenicians and the Persians, also shared many of the Mesopotamian myths.

▲ *A winged god, or "genie," holding a bucket and a pine cone. These objects were associated with purification. Images of genies were placed in buildings to protect people against demons and disease.*

Powerful gods

Mesopotamian civilizations were warlike. They produced a mythology in which powerful male gods destroyed the gods of the invader and inflicted cruel punishments on the people. Most of the female gods were weak by comparison, and they are rarely shown in Mesopotamian art. Heroes are always male; myths regularly involve violent battles with other men or monsters.

In most Mesopotamian cities, stepped brick towers called ziggurats were built. At the top were small temples, dedicated to the god that the city worshiped. Here the king, who was also the high priest, performed religious ceremonies and sacrifices.

There was a strong relationship between the king and his patron gods. For example, AHURA MAZDA is shown in Persian art with wings spread protectively over the kings. Art often shows the king making offerings to the gods, and both figures are shown at the same size. This suggests that they were equally important, since other members of society are smaller in scale. It may be the case that mythology was used to support the social structure.

As well as the gods, royal palaces were protected by the figures of fierce winged genies.

In Mesopotamia the land was dry, and irrigation was vital to grow crops. In a climate like this it is not surprising that the creation myth tells how, in the beginning, everything came from fresh water and salt water. From the mingled waters came two monstrous serpents who gave birth to Anshar, the sky, and Kishar, the Earth. In turn, sky and Earth gave birth to the gods. The gods then fought one another for control over the universe.

When human beings were finally created, they soon offended the gods with their bad behavior and were punished with a great flood. Only UTANAPISHTIM was warned in advance to build a boat and save his family and their animals. After seven days the terrible rain ceased and the boat settled on a mountaintop. Utanapishtim was blessed by the gods with immortality.

◀ In one scene from the Epic of Gilgamesh, *the hero battles with the Bull of Heaven, which* ISHTAR *had sent to destroy him.*

▲ *The Persian god* AHURA MAZDA *is a good spirit who battles forever with the evil Angra Mainyu. This is an example of the Persian belief that the force of good and the force of evil both exist in the world and are in eternal conflict.*

The Near Eastern myths spread westward when the Phoenicians established colonies in the western Mediterranean region. The growth of the Persian Empire helped the survival of Mesopotamian myths, although the Persians also developed new beliefs.

The longest and best-known Mesopotamian myth is the *Epic of Gilgamesh*. It tells the story of a king of Uruk and his search for eternal life. Recorded on 12 clay tablets, it was discovered during the 1800s by archaeologists.

▲ BAAL, *the young storm god, raises his mace to make the sound of thunder, and holds the lance which will unleash lightning.*

Although a fertility goddess, ANAT was once the cause of a drought. She desperately wanted a magic bow owned by a famous king. She offered him riches and even immortality, but the king would not part with it. In a fit of temper Anat killed the king, but the Earth fell barren at his death and the rain refused to fall until he was brought back to life.

ADAPA In Babylonian myth, the wise priest of the god EA. He liked to go fishing on the Euphrates River. One day a strong south wind caused his boat to capsize. He cursed the bird god of the wind and broke its wings. ANU, the supreme god, called Adapa to heaven to explain his behavior. Ea warned Adapa that he would be fed the bread and water of death, which he must refuse. In fact, Anu offered him the bread and water of life, and Adapa's refusal cost humanity the gift of eternal life.

■

AHURA MAZDA A powerful Persian god or good spirit who battles constantly against his opposite god, the evil Angra Mainyu. While Ahura Mazda is creator of all good things, such as fire and flowers, Angra Mainyu spoiled them by adding smoke and thorns. In the end, Ahura Mazda will defeat Angra Mainyu and all evil will be flushed from the world in a torrent of molten metal.

▼ *A Phoenician carving thought to show the popular fertility goddess* ASTARTE.

ANAT A Phoenician fertility goddess and the sister of BAAL. After Baal had been killed by MOT, Anat went down to the Underworld to plead for her brother's life. When Mot refused, she destroyed him in a fit of fury. Baal was revived and returned to Heaven. Mot also overcame death, and the story repeats itself each year, which explains Earth's annual cycle of decay in winter and renewal in the spring.

■

ANU The supreme Babylonian god of the sky. He lives apart from other gods and mortals on the highest summit of Heaven, where he eats and drinks the bread and water of eternal life. Anu was so remote that he was later replaced by his son ENLIL.

■

APSU *see* **TIAMAT**

■

ASSHUR The leading Assyrian god of war and husband of ISHTAR. He appears as an archer within a winged disk. When Assyria became more dominant, Asshur replaced the Babylonian god MARDUK as protector of the universe against chaos.

■

ASTARTE The Phoenician mother goddess who is visible from Earth as the planet Venus. Astarte was worshiped throughout the eastern Mediterranean as a fertility goddess of both love and war.

■

BAAL The god of storms who sends rain to water the crops. Baal is the son of EL. He defeated Yam, the sea god, with his mighty mace. Yam's death allowed people to sail the seas. The victory went to Baal's head, and he treated MOT disrespectfully. Mot summoned Baal to the Underworld, and made him eat the mud of death. The Earth would have turned into a desert if ANAT had not rescued Baal. His return to Heaven restored fertility to the soil.

EA (OR ENKI)   The Sumerian and Babylonian god of wisdom. His name means "of great intellect." Ea is one of the creators of humankind and the patron of the arts. He gave men and women the ability to reason. Ea constantly fought for divine power against his parents. In the end he overthrew his father, APSU, and took his place as god of fresh water.

■

EL   Supreme and all-knowing god of the Phoenicians. As creator of the universe he was known as "father of time." Like the Babylonian god ANU, he kept apart from other gods and mortals.

■

ENKI   see EA

■

ENKIDU   The heroic companion of GILGAMESH. He lived like a wild animal in the hills outside of Uruk, where Gilgamesh was king. Gilgamesh sent a woman to lure Enkidu into the city. After testing each other's strength in a wrestling match, they became friends and enjoyed many adventures together.

ENLIL   The Sumerian and Babylonian god of the air who brings both good and bad weather to the Earth. Enlil is one of the creators of humankind but grew weary of their noise and sent down a great flood to destroy them. EA warned a family, who built a boat and survived.

■

ERESHKIGAL   The Babylonian goddess of the Underworld. She was pulled from her throne by the war god, NERGAL, but instead of fighting they fell in love and agreed to marry and share their powers.

■

ETANA   A man chosen by the gods to be the first Sumerian king on Earth. He was childless and prayed to SHAMASH every day that he might be given a child. The god led him to an eagle, who took him to Heaven on its back in search of the plant of birth.

▼ ETANA *rescued an eagle from a deep pit, where it had been flung with broken wings as a punishment for eating the snake's children. Etana fed the bird and taught it to fly again, and as a reward the eagle took him to find the plant of birth.*

GILGAMESH The king of Uruk, a man of unrivaled strength and courage, and a renowned Babylonian hero. He went on many adventures with his friend ENKIDU and became so famous that the goddess ISHTAR wanted him to be her lover. When he refused, ANU punished him by sending down a plague which killed Enkidu. Gilgamesh became afraid of death and set out to find the secret of eternal life from UTANAPISHTIM. He returned without the secret and accepted his own mortality.

■

HADAD The son of ANU and the Assyrian god of storms and floods. He brought destruction to his enemies by sending down torrential rain to devastate their homes and crops. He brought wealth and prosperity to those who worshiped him by flooding the river plains each year to make their lands fertile.

■

INANNA The Sumerian goddess of both love and war, and the queen of Heaven. Inanna was obsessed with the Underworld because she wanted to test her powers against ERESHKIGAL, the goddess of the dead. As a condition of entry, Inanna had to shed an item of clothing at each of the seven doors of the Underworld, until she stood naked before the goddess of the dead. Inanna tried to pull Ereshkigal from her throne but failed, and was condemned to death. She saved herself by ordering her husband, Damuzi, to die in her place.

■

ISHTAR The Babylonian goddess of both physical love and war. She is closely identifed with INANNA and also descended to the Underworld, where she suffered a similar fate. She ordered her husband, TAMMUZ, to take her place with the dead. The Assyrians adopted Ishtar both as their goddess of war and as a wife for ASSHUR.

▼ *When* ISHTAR *was portrayed as the goddess of physical love, she was often shown naked or naked from the waist down. As a war goddess she appeared as a fearsome warrior who terrified even the gods. She was armed with every kind of weapon and accompanied by a lion, the symbol of ferocity.*

▶ NINURTA *was the only god brave enough to face the lionlike monster bird Anzu. They met on the side of a mountain. Ninurta called the winds to his aid and as the two faced each other, a storm raged about them. Ninurta killed the bird with an arrow tipped with poison.*

MARDUK Leading god of Babylon and the eldest son of EA. In the struggle for divine power between the gods and the first beings, TIAMAT AND APSU, only Marduk was brave enough to challenge Tiamat. She was the monster of chaos, but Marduk destroyed her, cut up her body, and created the universe from the pieces.

■

MOT The Phoenician god of death, infertility, and the Underworld. He is in constant conflict with BAAL. Each year, Mot summons Baal to die in the Underworld, and each time Mot is destroyed by ANAT, who grinds down his body and scatters it over the fields. Baal revives to restore fertility to the Earth, and Mot revives in time for the harvest.

TAMMUZ The Babylonian god of plants. He was the young husband of ISHTAR, who offered him to the Underworld in her place. Because the Earth is barren without him, each spring Ishtar arranges for his release, so that new crops can grow.

TIAMAT AND APSU The first beings, according to Babylonian mythology. Apsu was an abyss and the guardian of fresh water. Tiamat was the monster of chaos and represented salt water. They were the parents of the first gods but tried to kill their children because they made too much noise. In the terrible struggle that followed, Apsu was overthrown by EA, and Tiamat was slain by MARDUK, who created the Earth and sky from her body and established order.

UTANAPISHTIM A legendary Sumerian mortal who survived a great flood sent by ENLIL to punish humans. The grateful Utanapishtim made a sacrifice to the gods and was forgiven and made immortal by Enlil.

The Sumerian Moon god, Sin, is also the god of time because the waxing and waning of his light governs the passing of the months.

▼ *Worshipers pay homage to* SHAMASH. *He is seated behind an altar, which supports his symbol, the solar disk.*

NABU The son of MARDUK and the Babylonian god of wisdom, speech, and writing. He carries messages from the gods to mortals and taught humankind how to speak and write.

NERGAL The Babylonian god of war who led the gods into battle. Nergal became god of the dead when he wed ERESHKIGAL, who ruled the Underworld. Like MOT, he was an evil god who brought war and disease to the Earth in order to increase the numbers in his own kingdom.

NINURTA A Sumerian war god and the son of ENLIL. When nature rose up against Ninurta, he put down the rebellion and imposed order over chaos. Ninurta also taught mortals metalwork and pottery.

SHAMASH The Sumerian god of the Sun who flew across the sky by day. Since he could see everything on Earth, Shamash was also the god of justice.

· Egypt ·

To the ancient Egyptians, three things were more important than anything else: their king, the Nile, and the life in the next world. The Nile was the most important of the three. The river created fertile land in the middle of a great desert. Every year, it flooded and brought nourishing new soil to the farms by the side of the river. It was only because of the Nile that life could prosper.

This regular event was believed to be brought about by the gods. The Egyptians gave thanks to Osiris for the natural cycle of the seasons and to Isis for the gift of the flood.

Egyptian gods

In early times, before Egypt was one country under one ruler, each area had its own gods and goddesses. There were 42 districts, each with its own god, and even small towns had a temple dedicated to their god. After Egypt united, these gods were still followed, but they were not significant outside their own areas.

Other gods were important everywhere. The Egyptians were impressed by the great power of the Sun and sometimes saw it as an all-knowing eye that judged them. Ra, the Sun god, was one of the most important gods. He brought light and life to the world as he blazed across the heavens each day.

About 1353 B.C., the pharaoh Akhenaten insisted the Egyptians stop worshiping their numerous gods and worship only one god, Aten. He also made them worship him, as god king. After he died, the people went back to their old gods.

The Egyptians believed Ra was a creator figure who had mysteriously appeared from the waters of Nun. Ra's first creations were the gods of water and air. In turn, these produced the Earth and sky gods, Geb and Nut. The first human beings were formed from the tears of Ra, but on a later occasion he almost caused their destruction. When they dared suggest he was past his prime, he sent Sekhmet to punish them. The terrible slaughter was stopped just in time by the other gods.

Tefnut   Geb   Nut   Set   Nephthys   Shu

◄ *Egyptian gods and goddesses were sometimes shown with animal heads, such as the lion-headed* TEFNUT. *They also appear with animals that people connected with them.* GEB *is shown with a goose, because it is the hieroglyph (picture word) of his name. The gods are shown holding ankhs, symbols of life.*

Animal forms

Early Egyptians thought Ra and his fellow gods had the bodies of birds or animals. Ra himself was seen as a falcon. Other gods ranged from the cat goddess BASTET to Taweret, the goddess of childbirth who was usually shown as a pregnant hippopotamus.

Later, the gods took human bodies but retained their animal heads. Belief in animal gods sometimes led to bodies of animals being embalmed and buried in cemeteries.

The rising and setting of the Sun each day was seen as a sign from the gods that death was not final. The Egyptians believed that they continued to live in another world when they died. They carefully prepared for this by building strong stone tombs and decorating the walls with scenes of the life that they believed they would enjoy. Because it was thought that the body would come back to life in the tomb, their bodies were preserved by mummification.

► *The dead were helped by the* Book of the Dead, *instructions placed in their tomb to guide them through the afterlife. This illustration shows* THOTH, *the ibis-headed god who recorded the weight of the dead person's soul.*

◄ *The Egyptians buried their pharaohs with boats, so that they could travel to the next world. The royal tombs were also filled with food, the statues of servants, jewelry, and clothes to be enjoyed by the pharaoh in the afterlife.*

The Egyptians believed that their elaborate funeral rituals had been handed down to them from the gods. When Osiris was killed by SETH (*see page 76*), the jackal-headed god ANUBIS prepared the body for burial and carried out the funeral rituals. These became the basis of burial rituals from that point on. In Egyptian art, priests are sometimes shown wearing jackal-head masks.

▲ *In a temple of* AMEN-RA, *the chief priest offers the god food, incense, and flowers, while priestesses play musical instruments and sing hymns.*

▼ *The Nile god* HAPI *holds a tray laden with food, as a symbol of the life-giving river.*

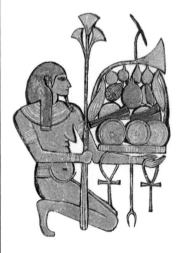

AMEN-RA Amen was a local god of the wind at Thebes in Upper Egypt. When Upper and Lower Egypt united under Theban rule, Amen gradually grew in importance and, in time, merged with RA to become the supreme god of Egypt.

■

ANUBIS The jackal-headed god of funerals and mummification. He protected the body while it was prepared for burial and continued to guard it in the tomb.

■

APIS The sacred bull of Memphis, and the god of strength and fertility.

■

ATEN A god of the Sun. Aten became the one and only god during the reign of the pharaoh Akhenaten, who believed that Aten created and controlled all things.

■

ATUM The god of the setting Sun, who merged with the Sun god RA to become Ra-Atum, the supreme god of Egypt. He was the chief of nine great gods worshiped in Lower Egypt.

BASTET A goddess who appeared as a cat. She was worshiped as the bringer of sunlight to the Earth.

■

BES The god of dancing and feasting, who was worshiped by the ordinary Egyptians. He appeared as a heroic dwarf wearing a lionskin and protected people from snakes and other harmful things.

■

GEB One of the group of nine great gods (the Great Ennead) worshiped at Heliopolis, or the "City of the Sun," in Lower Egypt. Geb was the Earth god.

■

HAPI The god of the Nile. Although male, Hapi had heavy female breasts. These were a symbol of humankind's dependence on the rich waters of the Nile for farming and nourishment.

■

HATHOR The goddess of love and fertility. She was shown either in the form of a cow or as a woman wearing a headdress in which a Sun disk was held between cow's horns. When RA sent her to destroy mortals, she changed into SEKHMET, the goddess of war and destruction.

HORUS The son of OSIRIS and ISIS, and god of the rising Sun. His great enemy was the evil SETH, who had seized the throne of Osiris. Horus challenged Seth for the throne, and they engaged in various contests of strength and cunning. In the end the outcome was decided by Osiris, who insisted that the throne was the rightful inheritance of Horus.

ISIS The goddess of love and destiny, and daughter of GEB and NUT. She married her brother OSIRIS, and their son was HORUS. Isis was a devoted wife and mother who used her magic powers to restore to life both Osiris and Horus after they had been killed by SETH. She is often portrayed nursing the infant Horus, whom she brought up to avenge the death of Osiris.

KHENSU or KHONS The son of AMEN-RA and MUT, and a god of the Moon. He gave power to the pharaoh and appeared as a handsome and virile youth, wearing a Moon on his head.

KHNEMU or KHNUM A potter god who created mortals from clay. His companion, Heqet, would then breathe life into them. Some say that they created the gods as well.

MAAT The daughter of RA and the goddess of justice and truth. She watched over religious rituals and checked that mortals were behaving themselves.

MENTHU or MONT The hawk-headed god of war. His sacred bull was Buchis, believed to be "the soul of RA."

MERETSEGER A local goddess of Thebes who appeared as a snake with a human head. She was kindly to the good but punished the bad with her poisonous bite.

MESKHENT The goddess of childbirth who helped women bear the pain of giving birth. Once the child was born she predetermined its future life.

MIN A virile fertility god associated with AMEN-RA. His followers performed a curious ritual of pole-climbing in his honor. He also protected the hunter-gatherer peoples who lived in the deserts east of the Nile.

MUT A mother goddess, shown wearing a vulture-headdress. When she married AMEN-RA, she became queen of Heaven.

NEFERTEM The son of PTAH and SEKHMET. He was shown as a bearded man who carried a curved sword and wore a lotus flower upon his head. In some texts, the Sun god RA emerged from a lotus each dawn.

▼ RA *had grown old and dribbled in his sleep.* ISIS *mixed earth with the saliva to make a snake that bit Ra. The old god was in terrible agony, which only Isis could cure. But she would not do so until he told her his secret name. This knowledge would make Isis the most powerful goddess, but Ra had no choice and whispered to her his real name.*

▼ The evil SETH *invited* OSIRIS *to a feast where a beautiful casket was on display. Osiris was offered the casket as a gift if he could fit inside. When Osiris climbed into it, Seth nailed down the lid and cast the casket into a river. It was eventually found by* ISIS *who used her magic powers to revive Osiris for long enough to father their son* HORUS.

NEITH   A goddess of domestic crafts who is said to have woven the world. She guarded the mummified body of dead people before they were buried.

■

NEKHBET   The wife of the Nile god HAPI and the patron of Upper Egypt. She acted as nurse to the royal children and appears as a vulture flying over the head of the pharaoh, whom she also protected.

■

NEPHTHYS   A goddess of the dead. When her husband SETH killed and hid the body of OSIRIS, Nephthys sided with her sister ISIS in her search for the corpse.

■

NUN   The god of the waters of chaos: an endless, shapeless deep that existed at the beginning of time in the dark before the universe was created. The first god, RA, magically emerged from Nun, who became known as the "father of the gods."

NUT   The goddess of the night sky and mother of the stars. She was the sister-wife of the Earth god GEB, but the two were so close that SHU split them apart.

■

OSIRIS   A fertility god who taught people how to farm the land and worship the gods. He was killed by his jealous brother SETH, who threw the body in a river. His mourning wife ISIS found the corpse and kept it hidden from Seth, but the body was discovered, and Seth cut it into pieces and scattered these across the Earth. Isis spent many months collecting the severed parts and made the body whole again. Osiris then became the god who judged the dead as they entered the Underworld.

■

PTAH   The local god of craftsmen and artists at Memphis in Lower Egypt. When Memphis became capital of Egypt, Ptah grew in importance and was said to have created the universe and the other gods.

■

RA   The original Sun god, who had the head of a falcon, and a solar disk and cobra as a headdress. He was the supreme creator, who made both gods and mortals. He was believed to be the father of every pharaoh.   (*See also* AMEN-RA *and* ATUM.)

■

RENENET   The goddess of babies and young children. She nourished them and gave them their names and fortunes.

■

RENPET   The goddess of the passing of the year, which she ushered in at spring, bringing vitality to all young people.

SEKER The god of vegetation and funerals. He appeared as a gruesome hawk-headed mummy who protected the gateway to the Underworld.

SEKHMET A formidable goddess of war who destroyed the enemies of RA. She began as HATHOR, the love goddess, but became the violent Sekhmet when Ra sent her to destroy all mortals.

SERAPIS A god of the Underworld who was worshiped by the Greeks and the Romans when they ruled Egypt. He was a mixture of APIS and OSIRIS and was said to be a healer with miraculous powers.

SESHAT The goddess of the written word who kept a library for the gods. She wrote down the past acts of mortals, and also wrote out their futures.

SETH The god of all evil things who murdered his brother OSIRIS and took his throne. The gods returned the throne to HORUS, whom Seth had been unable to kill. RA made Seth a storm god instead.

SHU The god of air and sunlight and the first creation of RA. When GEB and NUT lay in close embrace, SHU separated them and formed the Earth (Geb) below and the sky (Nut) above.

SOBEK The crocodile god of rivers and lakes. His followers believed him to be evil and made many sacrifices to him to make sure that he was kept happy.

TEFNUT The lioness-headed goddess of dew and rain and sister-wife of SHU.

THOTH The Moon god of magic and wisdom who was shown with an ibis head. He was the protector of speech and invented writing. He helped OSIRIS at the judgment of the dead by reading the scales as each soul was weighed.

UPUAT A jackal- or sometimes wolf-headed god, who guided the dead to the Underworld. He is linked with ANUBIS.

▲ *The Sun god* RA *rises each dawn and blazes across the sky in his boat. Toward the end of the day he grows old and at night he sails through the land of the dead. He emerges each morning refreshed and ready for a new day.*

Shai, the god of human destiny, is born with each child and travels with the child through life. When people die and enter the Underworld for judgment, Shai tells Osiris of every good and bad thing they have ever done.

· GREECE ·

The Greek creation myth describes how GAIA (the Earth) mysteriously appeared from the nothingness of space. By herself, she gave birth to URANUS (the sky), and together they were parents of the TITANS. These were the first gods. CRONUS, the youngest, deposed Uranus and became king of the sky. He married his sister Rhea, and they had six children.

However, fearing that he too would be overthrown by his own child, Cronus swallowed the first five children. Rhea managed to hide the sixth child, ZEUS, from him. The boy grew up in exile and eventually returned to challenge his father, forcing him to release the other children from his body. Zeus then led his brothers and sisters to victory in a war against the Titans. He exiled the Titans beneath the Earth and ruled from Mount Olympus with his brothers, sisters, and, later, his children.

Greek myths survived in the work of poets such as Homer, who wrote the *Iliad* and the *Odyssey* in the 700s B.C. These poems tell the story of the Trojan War, especially of ACHILLES, and of ODYSSEUS's long voyage home after the war ended.

The new gods

The Olympians were thought of as civilized powers who had conquered the barbaric Titans. This reflected the development of Greek society. From the 1100s B.C., the Greeks began to move out of their walled fortresses and develop cities. About six centuries later, Athens had become the center of Greek civilization and had replaced rule by tyrants with democracy —government by the people.

▶ *It took the new gods ten years to defeat the Titans in the battle to control the universe.*

78

Although the Olympian gods were immortal and enjoyed superhuman powers, they behaved in a human fashion. Zeus, for example, was god of justice, but he was certainly not a model of moral human behavior: he was often unfaithful to his wife and lost his temper. However, he was also seen as a heroic warrior who had brought about Greek civilization by destroying giants and monsters. The Greeks were therefore able to identify with the human as well as the heroic qualities of their gods.

The Golden Age

The ancient Greeks believed that there had once been a mythical "golden age." During this time the gods had lived happily with men on Earth, but the age had ended when men became greedy and fought causing the gods to leave in disgust. The gods then created PANDORA, the first woman, as a punishment.

Other Greek myths blamed JASON and THE ARGONAUTS for the collapse of the "golden age," because they had built the first boat and stolen the Golden Fleece. In her anger at this, the Earth refused to provide crops and cereals of her own accord, and people had had to learn how to farm the land.

The "age of bronze" followed—a time of heroic warriors whom the gods helped against their enemies. By the 700s B.C., the Greeks came to believe that their own time was an "age of iron." They thought the gods had almost entirely abandoned them and could be contacted only by prayers and sacrifice, or by a visit to an Oracle, where a priestess would advise them of the gods' will.

Myths were recited at feasts or religious festivals, or acted out in the theater. (The plays of Aeschylus and Sophocles are still performed today.) By telling stories in which the good were rewarded and the evil punished, the Greeks reinforced the values of their society.

▲ The gods made their will known through the Delphic Oracle. Pilgrims traveled long distances to visit this priestess of Apollo. She sat within the temple on a sacred tripod and, falling into a deep trance, answered all questions. Her replies were interpreted and written down by priests.

All over Greece, temples were built as homes for gods and goddesses. Athens is named after the goddess Athena and her temple was called the Parthenon. It once held a huge ivory and gold statue of her. The temple's ruins still stand above the city.

· ANCESTRY OF · THE GREEK GODS

In many of the world's mythologies, the family tree of gods and goddesses is quite complicated. This simplified chart shows how groups of Greek deities are related to each other. It also lists some groups of minor divinities, such as the Muses. Western culture has often drawn on ideas from Greek mythology and so some of these groups may be familiar to you already.

▼ ZEUS *inflicted terrible punishments on the Titans. This bowl shows* PROMETHEUS *bound to a post (it is usually a rock), while an eagle pecks at his liver. His brother* ATLAS *(left) is made to support the heavens on his shoulders.*

GAIA
The Earth and first being
See page 88

m

URANUS
The sky
See page 95

FIRST TITANS

CRONUS
Leader of the Titans
See page 85

m **RHEA**
Mother of ZEUS and the first Olympian gods

HYPERION
The Sun, later deposed by APOLLO

m **THEA**

CRIUS
Represents the power of the sea

m **Eurybia**

COEUS
With Phoebe, represents the evening light

m **PHOEBE**
With Coeus, represents the evening light

MNEMOSYNE
Represents memory

m **Zeus**

IAPETUS
Banished by Zeus to the deepest part of the Underworld

m **Clymene**
An Oceanid (a sea nymph fathered by Oceanus)

OCEANUS
Father of rivers, and source of all seas and streams

m **TETHYS**
"The nourisher," and mother of the water deities

THEMIS
Represents law and justice, and helped create humankind

m **Zeus**

First Olympian Gods

ZEUS *m* **HERA**
King of the gods
See page 95

m

Metis
An Oceanid, and
mother of ATHENA

HERA
Goddess of marriage
and childbirth, and
mother of ARES,
APHRODITE, and
HEPHAESTUS
See page 89

DEMETER
Goddess of grain
See page 86

HESTIA
Goddess of the
hearth and home
See page 89

HADES
God of the
Underworld
See page 88

POSEIDON
God of the Sea
See page 94

m

Amphitrite
A Nereid
See page 83

EOS
Goddess of the Dawn
See page 87

SELENE
Goddess of the Moon

HELIUS
God of the Sun

ASTRAEUS
Father of the stars and the
four winds

PALLAS *m* **Styx**
Father of the minor
gods Zelus (zeal), Cratus
(strength), Bia (force),
and Nike (victory)

Styx
Ruler of the Styx, the
river that surrounds
the Underworld

ASTERIA
Fleeing from Zeus, she fell
into the sea, forming the
island of Delos

LETO *m* **Zeus**
Escaping from Hera, fled
to Delos and gave birth
to APOLLO and ARTEMIS

▲ *A vase fragment
showing* POSEIDON
*wooing the sea
nymph,* AMPHITRITE.
*She swam away
at first, but was
brought back by
a dolphin.*

The Muses

CALLIOPE Epic poetry   **ERATO** Love poetry   **MELPOMENE** Tragedy   **TERPSICHORE** Dance   **URANIA** Astronomy
CLIO History   **EUTERPE** Music   **POLYHYMNIA** Hymns   **THALIA** Comedy

PROMETHEUS
The Titan who gave fire to
humankind
See page 94

ATLAS
The Titan who carried the
heavens on his shoulders
See page 84

EPIMETHEUS *m* **Pandora**
A Titan who foolishly
accepted Pandora as a
gift from Zeus

Pandora
The first woman
See page 93

River Gods

ACHELOUS

ASOPUS

STYX

DORIS *m* **Nereus**
Wise old man of the sea

EURYNOME *m* **Zeus**

The Nereids
Beautiful sea nymphs and attendants of
Poseidon

The Graces
Three beautiful attendants of Aphrodite

The Seasons
DIKE Justice
EIRENE Peace
EUNOMIE Order

The Fates
Three sisters whose
spinning controls the
destiny of humankind

CLOTHO Thread of life
LACHESIS Chance
ATROPOS Inevitability

The phrase "Achilles' heel," which is used to mean someone's weak or vulnerable spot, comes from the myth of ACHILLES, who could only be killed by a wound to the back of his heel.

In Greek mythology, heroes such as ACHILLES and AJAX are almost as important as the gods themselves. Indeed, the heroes are usually said to be the child of a god and a mortal parent, and this highlights that they are set apart from ordinary humans.

By the 400s B.C., people made offerings at shrines to a hero whose particular help they hoped to gain. These shrines were often built in places where the hero was supposed to have died or been buried.

ACHILLES   A great hero, who is the main character in *The Iliad*. When Achilles was a baby, his mother THETIS tried to make him invulnerable to injury by dipping him in the river Styx, but the heel by which she held him remained undefended. As he grew up, Thetis tried to prevent him becoming a warrior by disguising him as a girl, until ODYSSEUS unmasked him. Achilles was a leader of the Greek army during the siege of Troy *(see page 89)*. He later became a perfect example of bravery and athleticism to young Greeks.

■

ACTAEON   Actaeon was the most famous hunter in Greece. While out hunting one day in the woods, he spied on ARTEMIS bathing in a pool. She punished him by turning him into a stag, and he was hunted down by his own dogs.

■

ADONIS   An extremely handsome youth who was loved by APHRODITE herself. The goddess asked PERSEPHONE to look after him, but she too fell in love with him and refused to give him back. ZEUS decreed that they must share him, but ARES, Aphrodite's jealous lover, disguised himself as a wild boar and killed Adonis during a hunt.

■

AEOLUS   The king of the island of Aeolia, near Sicily, where he kept the winds imprisoned. ODYSSEUS borrowed the winds in a bag to speed his voyage home from the Trojan War. His sailors, believing the bag to contain treasure, opened it while Odysseus was asleep. The winds escaped and blew the ship off course.

■

AGAMEMNON   The king of Mycenae who led the Greek army during the Trojan War. When he arrived home, he was murdered by his wife CLYTEMNESTRA and her lover.

▲ When the hunter ACTAEON *spied on Artemis, she turned him into a stag. He was attacked by his own dogs.*

AJAX   A heroic warrior. During the Trojan War he was second only to ACHILLES in bravery, and the two were close friends. When Achilles was killed, Ajax demanded his armor for himself, but it was given to ODYSSEUS instead. Ajax went crazy with fury and committed suicide by falling upon his sword.

■

ALCESTIS   The wife of Admetus, the king of Pherae. When the FATES told her husband that he would become immortal if he could find someone to die in his place, all refused except Alcestis, who offered herself. She was later brought back from the Underworld by HERACLES.

■

AMAZONS, THE   A race of female warriors who lived near the Black Sea. They used men as slaves for breeding and housework, and if they gave birth to a male baby, they destroyed it. They were defeated by THESEUS when they invaded Athens.

AMPHITRITE An early goddess of the sea. When POSEIDON first asked her to marry him, she was reluctant to share her power and swam away to her brother ATLAS. Poseidon sent a dolphin to bring her back and they ruled the waves together.

ANCHISES A mortal who was the lover of the goddess APHRODITE. He boasted about her and was punished by ZEUS, who blinded him with a bolt of lightning. Anchises was the father of Aeneas, the Roman national hero. (*See page 98.*)

ANDROMEDA Andromeda's mother, Cassiopeia, the queen of Ethiopia, unwisely boasted that her daughter was more beautiful than the NEREIDS. As a punishment for her pride, POSEIDON sent a sea serpent to devour the Ethiopians. To appease the monster, Andromeda was chained to a rock as a sacrifice, but was rescued just in time by PERSEUS.

ANTAEUS The son of POSEIDON and GAIA. He forced strangers to wrestle with him and won every time because he drew his strength from contact with his mother, Earth. HERACLES defeated him by lifting him into the air.

ANTIGONE The daughter of OEDIPUS and Jocasta. She buried her brother Polynices, whose body had been forbidden a funeral by the Theban tyrant, Creon. To punish her defiance, Creon had her buried alive.

APHRODITE The goddess of beauty, love, and fertility. She was born from the foam of the sea and had the power to make every living thing fall in love, often against its will.

APOLLO The son of ZEUS and Leto and the twin brother of ARTEMIS. He was born on the island of Delos and became the god of the Sun, logic, and reason, a talented musician, a healer, and a hunter. Prophecies were made through his priestesses at the Delphic Oracle. Each winter he was said to leave Greece to travel far north to a region called Hyperborea. He returned in the spring, in a chariot pulled by white swans.

ARACHNE A mortal who foolishly dared to challenge ATHENA to a weaving contest. The goddess wove a tapestry showing her fellow gods as powerful beings, but Arachne showed them as weak and corruptible. Athena turned Arachne into a spider, doomed to spin and weave forever.

ARES The god of war. He was associated with the violent and bloody aspects of battle rather than heroic fighting, and for these reasons he was despised by both ordinary mortals and his fellow gods.

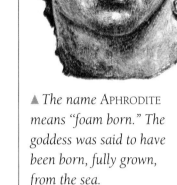

▲ *The name* APHRODITE *means "foam born." The goddess was said to have been born, fully grown, from the sea.*

▼ *During the Trojan War the* AMAZONS *came to the aid of Troy. Their queen, Penthesilea, was killed in battle by Achilles' spear.*

▼ *The Chimera was a fire-breathing monster who terrorized the people of Lycia.* BELLEROPHON, *mounted on the magical horse* PEGASUS, *destroyed him.*

ARGONAUTS, THE A group of heroes led by JASON. They sailed in the *Argo* from Greece to Colchis, at the other end of the Black Sea, and captured the Golden Fleece. On the way, the heroes had to row through the Clashing Rocks at the entrance to the Straits of Bosphorus. These were named because they crashed shut on any ship that tried to pass between them. The Argonauts sent a bird through the rocks first, then sailed through safely as the rocks reopened, before they could shut again.

ARIADNE The daughter of MINOS of Crete. She fell in love with THESEUS and helped him to kill her monstrous half-brother, the Minotaur. Despite this, Theseus abandoned her on the island of Naxos, where DIONYSUS fell in love with her and made her immortal.

ARTEMIS The daughter of ZEUS and Leto, and twin sister of APOLLO. She is the goddess of the Moon and watches over the purity of young people. She is also the goddess of the hunt.

ASCLEPIUS The son of APOLLO, he was a pupil of CHEIRON, the Centaur. He became such a talented doctor that he was able to bring the dead back to life. Consequently, ZEUS destroyed him because the Underworld was not being filled up fast enough. Asclepius became the god of medicine.

ATHENA The goddess of war and wisdom, and patron of arts and crafts. Athena was the warrior protector of Greek heroes and cities, especially Athens. She was born, fully grown, from the head of ZEUS. On her breastplate she wears the head of the GORGON, MEDUSA.

ATLAS A TITAN who led an unsuccessful war against the new Olympian gods and was severely punished by ZEUS. He was banished to the end of the world and forced to carry the heavens on his head and hands. The Atlas Mountains in northwest Africa are named after him.

BELLEROPHON The king of Lycia asked the young Corinthian prince Bellerophon to kill the Chimera, a beast made up of lion, goat, and snake. Flying above the monster on the back of the winged horse PEGASUS, he managed to destroy it. The king gave him his daughter in marriage as a reward. Later, while trying to reach the gods on Olympus, Bellerophon fell from Pegasus and was killed.

CASSANDRA A Trojan prophetess who was captured by AGAMEMNON. APOLLO had cursed her so that no one ever believed her prophecies (which were always right). She warned the Trojans not to pull the wooden horse into Troy; they ignored her and Troy fell to the Greek troops hidden inside the horse.

CASTOR AND POLLUX Also known as the Dioscuri, or "sons of Zeus," these twin heroes were born to LEDA. They sailed on the voyage of the ARGONAUTS and were later immortalized as the constellation known as Gemini or "the twins."

CENTAURS, THE Semiwild creatures who live outside cities. Although they are like men on the top half of their bodies, they are horses from the waist down. They were generally considered barbaric, but some, such as CHEIRON, were wise teachers of heroes.

CHARON The old gray-haired ferryman who takes the dead across the river Styx to HADES. Greeks were buried with a coin in their mouths to pay for his services.

CHARYBDIS A female monster in the shape of a whirlpool who lures ships toward her in the narrow straits between Italy and Sicily. If sailors try to avoid her, they must face the monster SCYLLA who lives opposite.

CHEIRON The wise old CENTAUR who taught the young ACHILLES, APOLLO, ASCLEPIUS, and JASON, as well as several other gods and heroes. He was also skilled in herbal medicine.

CIRCE A nymph with great magic powers. When ODYSSEUS and his men landed on her island, she changed the sailors into swine. Later she relented, and Odysseus and his men stayed with her as guests for one year.

CLYTEMNESTRA The daughter of LEDA and ZEUS, and wife of King AGAMEMNON of Mycenae. While Agamemnon was away fighting at Troy, she took his cousin Aegisthus as a lover and murdered the king when he returned. Her son ORESTES avenged his father by killing the couple.

CRONUS The son of URANUS and GAIA who ruled the TITANS. He killed his father and married his sister Rhea; however, he swallowed their children because he feared that one of them would destroy him. Rhea tricked Cronus into swallowing a rock in place of ZEUS, who indeed grew up and defeated him.

▲ *Although* CIRCE *had used her powerful magic to turn* ODYSSEUS's *men into pigs, he persuaded her to set them free. He was helped by Hermes, who gave him a plant that undid the spell.*

▲ DAEDALUS offended King Minos of Crete and was imprisoned with his son ICARUS. They escaped from prison with wings built from beeswax and feathers.

The first CYCLOPES were imprisoned by URANUS, the sky god, and rescued by ZEUS. They fought on Zeus's side during the battle against the Titans and gave him the weapons that helped the new gods win: thunderbolts for Zeus, a helmet of invisibility for Hades, and a trident for Poseidon.

CYCLOPES, THE   Originally three giant brothers, each with one eye in the middle of his forehead. Their descendants lived as shepherds in Sicily.

DAEDALUS   A highly skilled artisan and inventor from Athens. On the instructions of King MINOS of Crete, he designed a maze of corridors, known as the Labyrinth, as a home for the Minotaur.

DANAE   Danae was imprisoned by her father, Acrisius the king of Argos, who had learned that one day a grandson would kill him. ZEUS came to her in the form of a shower of gold and made love to her. She later bore him a son, the hero PERSEUS.

DAPHNE   APOLLO fell in love with the nymph Daphne. When she turned him down, he chased her through the woods, but she managed to escape him by turning into a laurel tree.

DEMETER   A daughter of CRONUS and Rhea who became the goddess of corn after her brother ZEUS took power. When her daughter PERSEPHONE was seized by HADES to live in the Underworld, Demeter wandered the Earth searching for her child, while plants withered and people died. Eventually Persephone was allowed to return to the Earth for six months each year. While she is away, it is winter.

DIONYSUS   The son of ZEUS and Semele, a Theban princess. To avoid HERA's anger, he was secretly brought up by nymphs. He returned to Greece in triumph as a young man in the strange company of MAENADS and SATYRS. He became god of vegetation, especially grapes and wine.

ECHO   A nymph who lived on Mount Helicon. ZEUS bribed her to keep his wife HERA occupied with constant chatter while he made love to other women. When Hera discovered the trick she punished Echo by allowing her only to "echo" the last words of others.

ELECTRA   The daughter of AGAMEMNON and CLYTEMNESTRA. When Clytemnestra and her lover murdered Agamemnon after his return from the Trojan War, Electra was forced to marry a peasant. She urged ORESTES to murder the adulterous couple.

ENDYMION   A handsome young king who caught the eye of Selene, the Moon goddess. She offered to grant him any wish if he slept with her. He chose to stay young forever by going to sleep for all time.

EOS   The beautiful goddess of the dawn, Eos fell in love with a young man called Tithonus and asked ZEUS to grant him immortality. Unfortunately, she forgot to ask that he stay young forever as well. When he became old and shriveled, she turned him into a grasshopper.

ERINYES, THE   Three terrifying female spirits, also known as the "Furies," who hound wrongdoers, especially anyone who has killed a relative. They were born from the blood of URANUS when CRONUS murdered him.

ERIS   The goddess of spite and quarrels. She arrived uninvited at the wedding of Peleus and THETIS, bringing a golden apple inscribed with the words "For the Most Beautiful." Three goddesses claimed the apple, but PARIS gave it to APHRODITE. Ultimately, this led to the Trojan War.

EROS   The young god of love who shoots people with gold-tipped arrows, causing them to fall in love forever.

EUROPA   A lovely Phoenician princess whose beauty attracted ZEUS. Disguised as a white bull, the god carried her across the sea to Crete where he made love to her. She gave birth to MINOS.

EURYDICE   When Eurydice died from a snakebite, her grieving husband ORPHEUS tried to fetch her back from the Under-world. He was allowed to lead her back to Earth on the condition that he did not look around as she followed him. He could not resist and she was lost to him forever.

FATES, THE   *see page 81*

EROS himself fell in love with the beauty of Psyche, a mortal. Since he could not let her know who he was, he always visited her in the dark. One night Psyche's curiosity got the better of her and she lit a candle to look at her sleeping lover. Hot wax fell on Eros, waking him, and he fled. In her search for him Psyche had to undergo many difficult tests before the two could be reunited.

▼ DEMETER, *the goddess of fertility, is helped by a young god called Triptolemus, who takes her gift of corn and the skill to grow it to people around the world.*

▲ HADES *ruled over the Underworld, which was divided into three lands. Very evil people were sent to Tartarus, where they suffered dreadfully for their past wrongdoing. The Asphodel Fields was a land of shadows, and most people went there after death. The golden Elysian Fields was the home of great heroes.*

A magical ram that was able to fly and speak once saved the Greek youth Phrixus from being sacrificed by his father. After carrying Phrixus to safety, the ram flew into the sky to become the constellation Aries. It left its golden fleece hanging on a sacred tree by the Black Sea, where it was later found by the ARGONAUTS.

GAIA The Earth goddess and one of the first beings to appear during the process of creation. She gave birth to the TITANS, but her husband, the sky god URANUS, pushed the children back inside her body, fearing that they would rebel against him. Gaia was avenged by her son CRONUS. She is also sometimes known as Ge.

■

GANYMEDE When Zeus saw the beautiful young Trojan prince Ganymede, he fell in love with him and sent an eagle to carry the boy to Mount Olympus. There he became an immortal and the cupbearer at divine banquets.

GORGONS, THE Three female monsters with golden wings, bronze hands, and poisonous snakes instead of hair. Just one glance from their terrifying faces has the power to turn people to stone. The gorgon MEDUSA was eventually killed by PERSEUS.

■

HADES The son of CRONUS and Rhea, and brother of ZEUS and the other Olympian gods. When Zeus divided the world into regions, Hades was given control of the Underworld, the kingdom of the dead, which he rules with his wife PERSEPHONE. Hades is also sometimes known as Pluto.

■

HARPIES, THE Female monsters in the shape of birds with human faces. They snatch food from tables as their victims eat and carry people from Earth to the ERINYES for punishment. Whenever someone went unaccountably missing, the Harpies were blamed by the Greeks.

■

HECATE At first a TITAN, she became the goddess of darkness and magic. She lives in the Underworld and, like DEMETER and PERSEPHONE, is said to bring fertility to the Earth. She is also seen as a figure of horror, who practices black magic and haunts tombs.

■

HECTOR The eldest son of PRIAM and Hecuba of Troy, and leader of the Trojan army. He was killed by ACHILLES, who then brought dishonor to Hector's body by dragging it behind his chariot three times around the walls of Troy.

■

HELEN A daughter of ZEUS and LEDA, and said to be the most beautiful woman in the world. She married King Menelaus of Sparta, but her beauty attracted the Trojan prince PARIS. She ran off with him, and this was the cause of the Trojan War.

HELIUS A TITAN and god of the Sun. Every morning he takes the Sun from beneath the eastern ocean, puts it in his chariot and rides to the top of the sky at noon. In the evening he disappears into the west and spends the night circling the ocean in a golden cup.

HEPHAESTUS The god of fire and all the crafts associated with it, including pottery and metalwork. He is the son of HERA and ZEUS, who one day threw him out of Olympus when he interfered in a quarrel between them. He fell to Earth and was crippled, but in the end he was welcomed back into Olympus.

HERA A daughter of CRONUS and Rhea. She married her Olympian brother ZEUS and became queen of the gods. As the goddess of marriage and childbirth she protects the rights of married women. Much of her time is spent punishing the lovers of Zeus and their children.

HERACLES The son of ZEUS and Alcmene, whom Zeus had made love to while disguised as her husband. Heracles proved his heroic qualities while still a baby when he strangled the snakes which HERA, angry with Zeus for his adultery, had sent to destroy him. Later Heracles successfully carried out twelve labors; these seemingly impossible tasks had been set as punishments for killing his own wife and children in a fit of madness inspired by Hera. When Heracles died he joined the gods on Mount Olympus.

HERMES As the messenger of the gods, Hermes uses his winged sandals and magic wand to fly from Olympus to Earth. He is allowed to enter the Underworld and takes people to Hades when they die. He is god of thieves and moneymakers.

HESTIA The eldest child of CRONUS and Rhea; she is the popular goddess of the hearth, home, and family.

During his twelve labors, Heracles fought a number of fantastic beasts. The Stymphalian Birds lived hidden among the reed beds of Lake Stymphalus and fed on the local people. Heracles used a giant rattle to scare them out and then shot them with his arrows. The Hydra grew two heads for every one lopped off by Heracles. He eventually defeated it by applying a burning torch to the wounds. His final labor was to bring the three-headed watchdog Cerberus out of the Underworld, where it guarded the gates against living beings.

THE TROJAN WAR

The story of the Trojan War is famous. The war was caused by HELEN eloping with PARIS to Troy and was fought between the Greeks and the Trojans.

The Greeks laid siege to Troy for ten years before ODYSSEUS thought of making a giant wooden horse, in which a few Greek warriors could hide. The horse was left outside the city walls as a token of defeat, and the Greek army pretended to sail away. The Trojans, believing they had won, dragged the horse into the city. During the night the hidden warriors slipped out from the horse and opened the city gates for the waiting Greek army. Troy was totally destroyed.

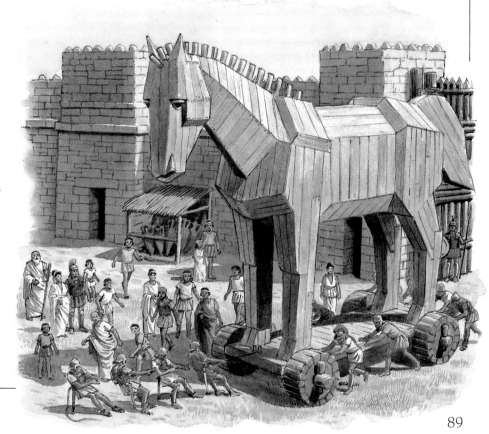

▲ JASON *needed Medea's help to capture the Golden Fleece. The fleece was kept in a sacred grove and guarded by a fierce dragon that never slept. Medea prepared a magic potion which Jason scattered over the dragon. It fell into a deep sleep, and Jason was able to seize the Fleece.*

HIPPOLYTUS Hippolytus was the son of THESEUS and Hippolyta, an AMAZON queen. Phaedra, Theseus's wife, fell in love with her stepson. But Hippolytus rejected her and she hanged herself, leaving a spiteful note claiming that he had raped her. Theseus prayed to POSEIDON to punish his son, and the god sent a bull from the sea, causing the innocent Hippolytus to crash his chariot and die.

■

ICARUS As a boy, Icarus learned craft skills from his father, DAEDALUS. The pair were imprisoned by King MINOS of Crete, but escaped by fixing wings made with feathers and beeswax to their arms. As they flew, Icarus, exhilarated by the experience, forgot his father's warning and recklessly went too close to the Sun. The wax in his wings melted and he crashed to his death in the sea.

IO When ZEUS fell in love with Io, he turned her into a cow to keep the affair secret from HERA. Hera nonetheless learned the truth and sent the many-eyed giant Argus to guard Io, but HERMES killed this watchman. Hera then sent a gadfly to sting Io, making her run away from Zeus to Egypt where the god finally caught up with her.

■

IPHIGENIA When AGAMEMNON killed deer sacred to ARTEMIS, the goddess made him sacrifice his daughter Iphigenia before she would allow the Greeks to sail to war against Troy. Some say that Artemis substituted a deer at the last moment, making Iphigenia her special priestess.

■

IRIS The messenger of the gods and goddess of the rainbow.

■

IXION Ixion, the king of the Lapiths, was invited to dine on Mount Olympus. He dared to flirt with HERA. ZEUS turned a cloud into Hera's image, and Ixion made love to it. He was punished by being tied to a fiery wheel and will roll through the Underworld for the rest of time.

■

JASON Jason was the heir to the throne of Iolcus, but his uncle Pelias cheated him of his inheritance and the boy grew up in exile. When Jason became a man, he went back to claim his throne, but Pelias insisted that before he could be heir he must bring the Golden Fleece from Colchis. Jason led the ARGONAUTS on this quest. The princess Medea fell in love with him when he arrived in Colchis and betrayed her father by helping Jason to obtain the Fleece. The pair went to Corinth, where Jason abandoned Medea for Glauce. Medea took revenge on him by killing Glauce. She then escaped to Athens.

LEDA ZEUS fell in love with Leda and made love to her disguised as a swan. Out of the fertilized egg were born CASTOR AND POLLUX, CLYTEMNESTRA, and HELEN.

MAENADS The female followers of DIONYSUS. They dressed in animal skins and worshiped the god in wild dances, often encouraging mortal women to join them against the will of their husbands.

MEDUSA One of the GORGONS. PERSEUS cut off her head, using his polished shield as a mirror to avoid gazing into her eyes and being turned into stone. He awarded the head to the goddess ATHENA, who wears it on her breastplate.

MIDAS King Midas of Phrygia wore a turban to hide the fact that he had ass's ears—inflicted on him by APOLLO when the king voted for PAN in a musical contest. Midas was once granted a wish by DIONYSUS and wished that everything he touched might be turned to gold. But when his food and even his daughter turned to gold, the unhappy king regretted his greed. Finally Dionysus lifted the magic spell.

MINOS The son of EUROPA and ZEUS who became king of Crete. POSEIDON made Minos's wife, Pasiphae, fall in love with a bull, with whom she had a child, half man and half bull, called the Minotaur. DAEDALUS built a maze, called the Labyrinth, as a home for the monster, who was fed on young Athenians before THESEUS killed him with the help of Minos's daughter, ARIADNE.

▶ THESEUS *killed the Minotaur and escaped from the Labyrinth, guided by the thread from a ball of twine.*

MUSES, THE *see page 81*

NARCISSUS A beautiful Greek youth who spurned the love of others. When ECHO fell in love with him, he ignored her until she faded away with grief—only her voice lingered on. After this, ARTEMIS punished Narcissus by making him fall in love with his own reflection in a pool. He tried in vain to hold the image but died of a broken heart. He was turned into the beautiful flower that bears his name.

NEMESIS The goddess of divine revenge. She punishes people who show too much pride or who have too much undeserved good luck, as well as those who perform evil actions. She was often shown with a scales in one hand and a whip in the other.

NEREIDS, THE   *see page 81*

NIOBE   The daughter of TANTALUS, Niobe boasted that her children were more beautiful than the children of Leto, APOLLO, and ARTEMIS. In revenge they killed Niobe's children with their arrows. The grieving mother was transformed into a weeping stone.

ODYSSEUS   A Greek hero, renowned for his cunning intelligence, who fought at Troy. It took him ten years to sail home to Ithaca, a small island in the Ionian Sea, because he was obstructed by POSEIDON, whom he had offended. During the voyage he had many adventures with monsters and magicians. He alone survived the journey; all his men drowned in a shipwreck when they ate the sacred cattle of Hyperion. When he eventually reached home, disguised as a beggar, he killed the hundred suitors who had pursued his faithful wife, PENELOPE.

OEDIPUS   Oedipus was the son of Laius and Jocasta, the rulers of Thebes. King Laius was told that his son would one day kill him, so the baby Oedipus was left on a hillside to die. He was rescued, however, and grew up in the Corinthian court. Not knowing who he was, he fulfilled the prophecy when he killed his father and married his mother. As punishment, the gods sent a plague to Thebes. When he learned the truth of his birth, Oedipus blinded himself and went into exile.

ORESTES   The son of AGAMEMNON and CLYTEMNESTRA. He left home while Agamemnon fought at Troy. When he heard that his father had been murdered by Clytemnestra and her lover, Orestes returned and killed the pair in revenge.

ORION   A giant hunter whose father, POSEIDON, gave him the power to walk across the sea. When ARTEMIS fell in love with him, her jealous brother APOLLO one day pointed to a speck out at sea and challenged her to hit it with her arrows. She succeeded but discovered too late that she had hit Orion. Artemis turned the hunter into a constellation that appears to walk on the waves.

ORPHEUS   Orpheus was taught to play the lyre by his father, APOLLO. He then introduced poetry and music to human beings. His own playing was so beautiful that rocks danced to his music. Orpheus died when MAENADS tore him to pieces.

PAN   The god of wild nature, shepherds, and their flocks. He has goat's horns and plays his pipes to enchant animals. Pan can make animals and people feel suddenly terrified. Our word "panic" derives from Pan.

▼ ORPHEUS *played the lyre so beautifully that he charmed the spirits of the Underworld to allow him to reach his dead wife Eurydice. But as he led her up to Earth, he disobeyed the instruction not to look back, and she was lost to him forever.*

PANDORA The first woman. She was created by ATHENA and HEPHAESTUS and given to men by ZEUS as punishment for accepting fire from PROMETHEUS. Pandora brought with her to Earth a jar filled with evils that she allowed to escape into the world; only Hope was left in the jar. We still use the phrase "Pandora's box" to describe a troublesome situation.

PARIS The son of PRIAM and Hecuba of Troy. He judged APHRODITE to be the most beautiful goddess and in return she gave him HELEN, the most beautiful mortal woman. Paris took Helen from her husband, Menelaus of Sparta, and this act led to the Trojan War. Paris died on the battlefield after killing ACHILLES.

PEGASUS A magical winged horse that sprang out of the neck of MEDUSA when PERSEUS cut off her head. He was ridden by BELLEROPHON until the hero tried to fly to Olympus. The gods sent a gadfly to sting the horse, who threw Bellerophon back to Earth. Pegasus then became a carrier of thunderbolts for ZEUS.

PELOPS Pelops fell in love with Hippodamia, but before he could marry her he had to compete in a chariot race with her father, King Oenomaus. Pelops won the race and founded the Olympic Games on the spot where the race began.

PENELOPE The wife of ODYSSEUS. When her husband went to Troy she was pestered by suitors, who tried to convince her that he was dead. She replied that she would marry one of them when she had finished weaving a shroud for her father-in-law. But at night she unraveled what she had made by day, and so kept the suitors waiting until Odysseus returned.

PERSEPHONE When HADES carried Persephone off to the Underworld, DEMETER's grief was so great that the girl was eventually allowed to spend half the year with her mother on Earth. Each spring she returns, filling the world with flowers and fruit. In the winter she stays with Hades, and the fields are bare.

PERSEUS The son of ZEUS and DANAE. He grew into a hero and killed the GORGON, MEDUSA, presenting her head to ATHENA who wore it on her breastplate as a weapon—it turned anyone who looked at it to stone. Perseus married ANDROMEDA after freeing her from a sea monster.

PHAETON Phaeton was the son of HELIUS. He once borrowed the Sun chariot from his father, but in his inexperience lost control of the horses as they neared the top of the sky. To save the Earth, ZEUS hit Phaeton with a thunderbolt and he crashed into the sea and died.

▲ PERSEUS *returned with Medusa's head to the island of Seriphos, where he and his mother, Danae, were guests of King Polydectes. He was furious to discover that the king was trying to force himself on Danae. Holding up Medusa's head, Perseus turned the king and his court to stone.*

▲ *As the hungry* TANTALUS *stretched for the succulent fruit above his head, it moved just out of reach. As he tried to drink from the pool, the water receded from his pursed lips. The word "tantalize" comes from his punishment.*

Pygmalion was a king of Cyprus who could find no mortal woman beautiful enough to marry. He carved a female statue out of ivory and fell in love with it. Aphrodite answered his prayers and turned the statue into a real woman.

POSEIDON The god of the sea, horses, and earthquakes. His brother ZEUS gave him the sea as his kingdom after the TITANS were defeated by the Olympians. Poseidon uses the power of his trident (given to him by the CYCLOPES) to stir up storms at sea.

PRIAM A king of Troy, who was killed when the Greeks finally entered the city after a ten-year siege. Priam wished to end the war by returning HELEN to her home, but his sons PARIS and HECTOR argued to keep her at Troy.

PROMETHEUS The son of the TITANS Iapetus and Clymene. After the battle with the Olympians he became the champion and benefactor of human beings. He stole fire from the gods and gave it to mortals but was punished by ZEUS by being tied to a rock for eternity and pecked by an eagle.

SATYRS The male followers of DIONYSUS. They have human bodies, with horses' tails and pointed ears. Their animal natures lead them to drunkenly chase nymphs and MAENADS through the woods whenever they have time off from helping Dionysus with his wine-making.

SCYLLA Scylla was once a beautiful sea nymph who made jealous CIRCE angry when a sea god fell in love with her. Circe turned Scylla into a monster with a woman's head and torso, but with six dogs attached to her body instead of legs. Scylla lives in a cave opposite the whirlpool of CHARYBDIS. Whenever sailors avoid the whirlpool, Scylla grabs and eats them.

SILENUS The oldest of the SATYRS and foster father of DIONYSUS. He has receding hair and the potbelly of an old drunkard.

SIRENS The sirens have the upper halves of women and lower halves of birds. They lure sailors to their deaths by singing enchanting songs. On his voyage home, ODYSSEUS was tied to his ship's mast so that he could hear their song while his sailors blocked their ears with beeswax.

SISYPHUS A king of Corinth who tried to cheat death and informed on ZEUS when the god committed adultery. His punishment is to spend eternity in the Underworld rolling a boulder up a hill which rolls back down whenever he has nearly reached the top.

SYRINX Syrinx was a woodland nymph, with whom PAN fell in love and chased. Just as he caught up with her by a river, she cried to the water nymphs for help. They transformed her into reeds, and Pan made these into "panpipes."

TANTALUS The king of Sipylos and a son of ZEUS. Tantalus was always welcome at the feasts of the gods—until he tried to test how all-knowing they were by serving his son PELOPS as the main course. The gods were wise to the trick and restored Pelops. They punished Tantalus by placing him in an Underworld pool, where food and drink are just out of his reach and he will remain forever hungry and thirsty.

TELEMACHUS The son of ODYSSEUS and PENELOPE. When Odysseus left for Troy, Telemachus was too young to fight the suitors who tried to press his mother into marriage. As a man he went in search of Odysseus, who eventually returned. Together they killed all the suitors.

THESEUS The son of King Aegeus of Athens, although some say that POSEIDON was his true father. Theseus admired the heroic acts of HERACLES and grew up to become a great hero himself. Like Heracles, Theseus killed many monsters and villains. After killing the Minotaur with the help of ARIADNE, he sailed back to Athens but forgot to change the black sail on his ship to a white one as a signal to Aegeus that he had been successful. Aegeus saw the black sail and jumped to his death; Theseus then became king.

THETIS A sea nymph. The mortal Peleus fell in love with her, but she avoided his advances by turning herself into various slippery animals. Peleus eventually caught her. Their son was the hero ACHILLES.

TIRESIAS An aged prophet who offended the gods and was struck blind. He was famous for his ability to see hidden truths and warned OEDIPUS that he had killed his father and was sleeping with his mother.

TITANS, THE *see page 80*

URANUS The first god of the sky. He feared that one of his children would grow up and destroy him, so he pushed the babies back into the body of his wife, GAIA. His son, CRONUS, eventually destroyed his power with Gaia's help.

ZEUS The king of the Olympian gods and god of justice. His father, CRONUS, had been told that one of his children would destroy him, as he had destroyed his own father, so Cronus swallowed his babies. When Zeus was born his mother gave Cronus a rock to swallow and the child was secretly raised by some nymphs. When he became a man, Zeus gave Cronus a potion that made him cough out Zeus's sisters and brothers. Together they defeated Cronus and the TITANS, and Zeus became king of the new gods on Mount Olympus, wielding thunderbolts against his enemies.

HERA's jealousy makes life very dangerous for ZEUS's lovers. In one story, the goddess persuaded Semele, a Theban princess who was expecting Zeus's child, to ask the god that he appear to her in his real form; his thunderbolts destroyed her. Zeus saved the child, DIONYSUS, by sewing him into his thigh until he was ready to be born.

▼ HERACLES, *escorted by* ATHENA, *the patron of heroes, is welcomed to Olympus as an immortal by his father,* ZEUS.

· ROME ·

The Romans believed that their nation had been founded by a Trojan warrior called AENEAS. When the Greeks destroyed Troy, Aeneas escaped the burning city and finally arrived in Italy after a long and dangerous voyage across the Mediterranean. His mother, the goddess Venus, provided him with the protection of the gods and guidance to reach his promised land.

The city of Rome

According to legend, Rome was founded in 753 B.C. by ROMULUS and Remus, twin brothers who were descendants of Aeneas. The twins quarreled over who should rule Rome, and Romulus killed his brother and became the first king.

Six centuries later, Rome conquered Greece and absorbed much of Greek mythology by importing works of art and literature. Roman mythology was a mixture of myths and legends from both the Greek and Roman worlds.

The Romans adopted the Greek myths, and many of the Greek gods and goddesses were combined with Roman deities. Major Roman figures are listed below, with their Greek equivalents in brackets.

JUPITER: the chief god (ZEUS)
JUNO: the queen of the gods (HERA)
MINERVA: the goddess of science and wisdom (ATHENA)
PLUTO: the god of the Underworld (HADES)
NEPTUNE: the god of the sea (POSEIDON)
BACCHUS: the god of wine and fertility (DIONYSUS)
DIANA: the goddess of hunting (ARTEMIS)
VENUS: the goddess of love (APHRODITE)
APOLLO: the god of light, healing, and music (APOLLO)
CERES: the goddess of agriculture (DEMETER)
MARS: the god of war (ARES)
VULCAN: the god of metalwork (HEPHAESTUS)
CUPID: the god of love (EROS)
MERCURY: the messenger of the gods (HERMES)

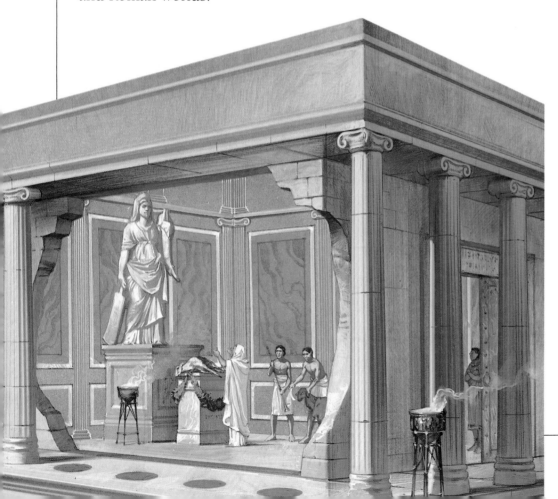

◄ There were a great many temples in Rome, and each was dedicated to a particular god or goddess. At the temple, sacrifices were offered in order to persuade the divine power to grant a particular request.

▲ The Roman senate pronounced many of the emperors to have become gods after their death.

Roman legends

Although the major Roman gods were believed to be the same as Greek gods, there were certain popular legends, as well as gods, that the Romans proudly regarded as part of their own native tradition.

For example, unlike the Greeks, the Romans believed that their empire had been created by the heroic deeds of real human beings rather than demigods. Aeneas is therefore represented as a man with real feelings and human failings.

Women also play a major role in the early legends. Lucretia, who killed herself when raped by a son of the tyrant Tarquin, became seen as the perfect example of female honor.

The Romans were very superstitious. They believed that "genii," or spirits, were present in both the town and the country and needed to be kept happy at all times.

Each family worshiped various household gods. The PENATES were protectors of the storeroom, and therefore the family's wealth. The LARES brought wealth and happiness to the family. Every day, offerings of wine, cakes, and incense were made to these gods at household shrines. These often contained statues of a lar, wearing a tunic and holding a drinking horn and a bowl.

The family "genius" was the name for the spirit of the male head of the household. The genius was worshiped by all the family, including the slaves. There were also state lares who were worshiped in public ceremonies as protectors of the Roman nation. The emperor was the state genius. Neglecting any of these gods might lead to disaster for state or household.

As the Roman empire grew, many foreign gods and myths were tolerated, and sometimes even became part of Roman beliefs. Worship of the Persian figure MITHRAS, for example, spread quickly.

▼ After a bull was sacrificed to the gods, a priest examined its liver for signs that the god or goddess had accepted the offering.

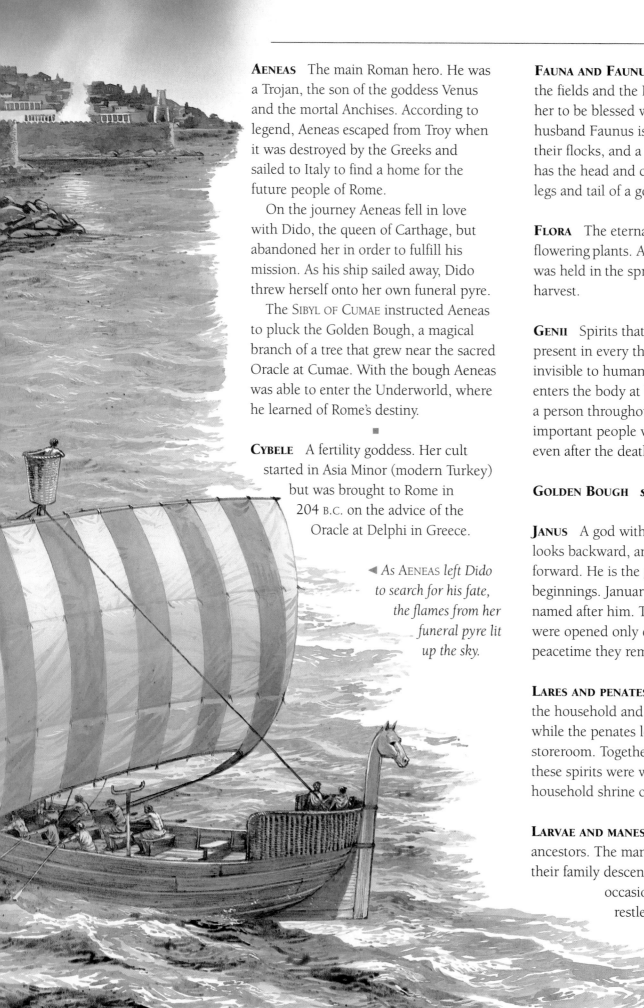

AENEAS   The main Roman hero. He was a Trojan, the son of the goddess Venus and the mortal Anchises. According to legend, Aeneas escaped from Troy when it was destroyed by the Greeks and sailed to Italy to find a home for the future people of Rome.

On the journey Aeneas fell in love with Dido, the queen of Carthage, but abandoned her in order to fulfill his mission. As his ship sailed away, Dido threw herself onto her own funeral pyre.

The SIBYL OF CUMAE instructed Aeneas to pluck the Golden Bough, a magical branch of a tree that grew near the sacred Oracle at Cumae. With the bough Aeneas was able to enter the Underworld, where he learned of Rome's destiny.

■

CYBELE   A fertility goddess. Her cult started in Asia Minor (modern Turkey) but was brought to Rome in 204 B.C. on the advice of the Oracle at Delphi in Greece.

◀ As AENEAS *left Dido to search for his fate, the flames from her funeral pyre lit up the sky.*

FAUNA AND FAUNUS   Fauna is goddess of the fields and the Earth. Women prayed to her to be blessed with fertility. Her husband Faunus is god of shepherds and their flocks, and a god of prophecy. He has the head and chest of a man, but the legs and tail of a goat.

■

FLORA   The eternally youthful goddess of flowering plants. A festival to honor Flora was held in the spring to ensure a rich harvest.

■

GENII   Spirits that were believed to be present in every thing and place, but invisible to human beings. The genius enters the body at birth and watches over a person throughout life. The genii of important people were often worshiped even after the death of the person.

■

GOLDEN BOUGH   *see* **AENEAS**

■

JANUS   A god with two faces: one that looks backward, and one that looks forward. He is the god of doorways and beginnings. January, the first month, is named after him. The doors of his temple were opened only during war—during peacetime they remained shut.

■

LARES AND PENATES   The lares protect the household and its surrounding land, while the penates look after the house storeroom. Together with the family GENII, these spirits were worshiped at a household shrine called the lararium.

■

LARVAE AND MANES   The spirits of dead ancestors. The manes were worshiped by their family descendants on special occasions. The larvae were restless and haunted the living as ghosts.

LAVINIA The daughter of King Latinus of Latium, and the granddaughter of FAUNUS. She married AENEAS after he killed Turnus, the man she was engaged to marry. It is said she gave the Romans Latin, the language of her people.

MITHRAS An Iranian god who became very popular with the Romans after they had conquered the eastern Mediterranean. Mithras is often shown as a young man in the act of killing a massive bull (bull sacrifice was a central part of his cult). His followers believed that he offered the chance of life after death to those of his followers who died heroically. As a result, he was often worshiped by Roman soldiers in elaborate ceremonies, which women were not allowed to attend.

PENATES *see* **LARES**

ROMULUS According to legend, the founder of Rome in 753 B.C. As babies, he and his twin brother Remus were thrown in the Tiber River by their mother, Rhea Silvia, a virgin priestess who had been raped by the war god Mars. The twins came to shore on the site of future Rome, where they were cared for by a wolf until a shepherd discovered them and brought them up. The twins set out to form a new city together, but Romulus killed Remus in a violent quarrel and ruled alone.

SIBYL OF CUMAE A prophetess who lived in a cave at Cumae in Italy. She guided AENEAS on his journey to the Underworld, where he saw the future of the Roman people. Her prophecies were recorded in books and kept in a temple in Rome.

VESTA The goddess of the hearth. Vesta had a round temple in the Roman Forum, in which her eternal sacred flame was kept alight by the Vestal Virgins.

▲ *In Roman art, CYBELE is sometimes shown seated beside the shepherd boy Attis in a chariot pulled by lions. Her worship sometimes involved wild music and dancing.*

ROMULUS is said to have disappeared in a whirlwind. Later, he appeared to a Roman citizen in a dream and explained that he had been kidnapped to join the gods. The Romans worshiped him as the god Quirinus.

·EASTERN ASIA·

Eastern Asia is home to some of the oldest cultures and mythologies in the world. In China some myths can be traced back nearly 4,000 years. In India, parts of the sacred mythological texts were composed before 1000 B.C. The ancient myths and legends of Hinduism and Buddhism are the most influential and widespread in the region, and today are as vibrant as ever. Both originated in India. While Hindu mythology spread south through Myanmar (Burma) and Southeast Asia, Buddhist tales were carried east to Japan.

Local myths have always existed alongside the great Buddhist or Hindu traditions. Beliefs in spirits and ghosts are widespread, and mythological animals derived from the snake or the dragon are found all over Asia. Many of the original myths in Asia probably changed with the introduction of Buddhism and Hinduism. More recently, local myths may have changed through contact with Christian and Islamic beliefs.

Asian myths are often very complex. In India the gods take on many different forms and aspects, and in China hundreds of gods are found on Earth, in Heaven, and in the Underworld. In Chinese and Japanese mythology the characters can move from one realm to the other, but generally in Indian mythology the gods stay in Heaven. Ancestor myths are significant on the islands of Southeast Asia, China, and Japan, but do not seem to exist in India.

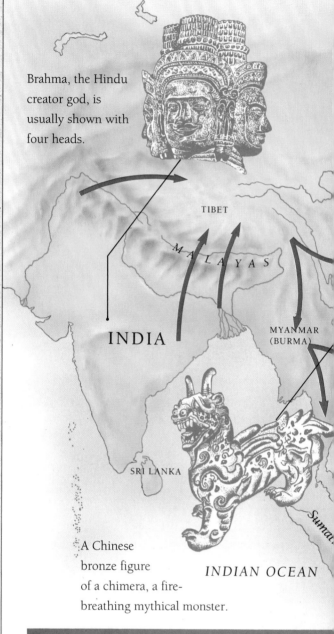

Brahma, the Hindu creator god, is usually shown with four heads.

TIBET

MALAYAS

INDIA

MYANMAR (BURMA)

SRI LANKA

Sumatra

INDIAN OCEAN

A Chinese bronze figure of a chimera, a fire-breathing mythical monster.

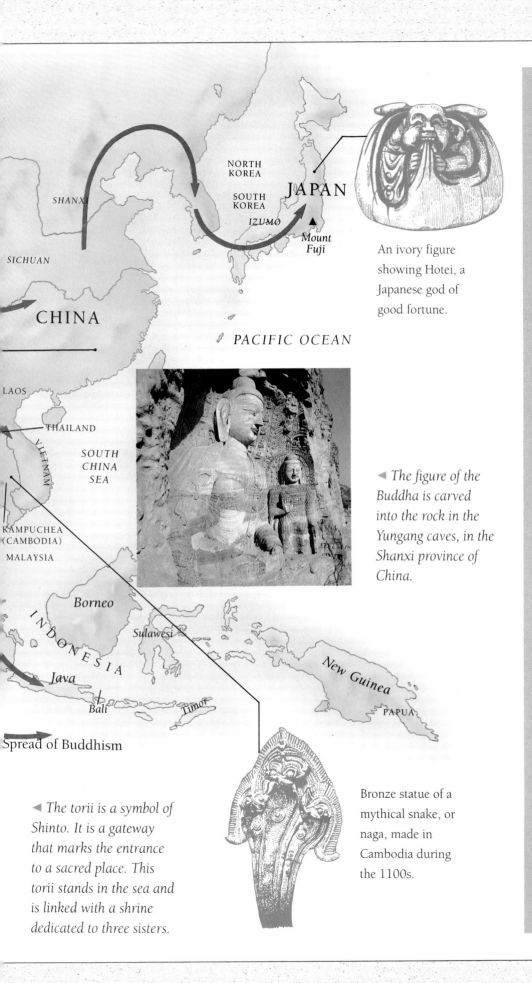

An ivory figure showing Hotei, a Japanese god of good fortune.

PACIFIC OCEAN

◄ *The figure of the Buddha is carved into the rock in the Yungang caves, in the Shanxi province of China.*

Spread of Buddhism

◄ *The torii is a symbol of Shinto. It is a gateway that marks the entrance to a sacred place. This torii stands in the sea and is linked with a shrine dedicated to three sisters.*

Bronze statue of a mythical snake, or naga, made in Cambodia during the 1100s.

·INDIA·

Hinduism, the major Indian religion, is one of the oldest living faiths, with roots that go back thousands of years. Over 805 million people worldwide are Hindu. Unlike Buddhism or Christianity, Hinduism did not stem from the teachings of one man, but developed gradually over thousands of years and was influenced by many cultures and religious beliefs. As a result, it is a very complex religion with a rich range of mythology.

The basis of Hinduism is found in its sacred writings. The earliest of these is a collection of sacred songs and hymns called the *Vedas*. This word can be translated as "books of knowledge." They were composed over 3,000 years ago, but for a long time were thought too sacred to write down. The gods found in these early hymns are known as the Vedic gods. They represent powers of nature, such as VARUNA, a god of the sky, seas, and waters. The chief god in the *Vedas* is the warlike INDRA.

Hinduism includes veneration of the Sun, Earth, and sky. Hindus believe in reincarnation—that when someone dies, the soul moves into the body of someone or something else; who or what depends on actions in the previous life.

Brahma, Vishnu, and Shiva

The religious beliefs of the *Vedas* developed gradually into Hinduism. The Vedic gods were replaced in importance by a new group: the "trimurti" of BRAHMA, VISHNU, and SHIVA. They are the main gods of later Hinduism and are said to be three different forms of Brahman, the universal spirit.

Many of the characters in Hindu mythology overlap and are related to each other. Certain gods, such as Vishnu, have taken on different forms or manifestations—these are known as "avatars." Vishnu has appeared on Earth to help humankind in nine forms so far; his most popular avatars are RAMA and KRISHNA.

◄ *The* Mahabharata *is an important Hindu poem. In one part of the epic, an army commander lectures to his listeners on good government as he lies dying of his battle wounds.*

The *Mahabharata*

The stories of some of the most important Hindu heroes appear in an epic poem, called the *Mahabharata*. This dates from 400-300 B.C. It describes the war between two families, the Pandawas and the Korawas.

Much of the action centers on the hero ARJUNA. The poem is a story of the fight between good and evil, with good finally triumphant. The most popular passage of the epic is the important philosophical poem, called the *Bhagavad-Gita*, which means "Song of the Divine One."

The *Ramayana* is another important poem. It describes the adventures of Rama, an avatar of Vishnu, as he searches for his bride SITA, who has been kidnapped by RAVANA, the fearsome demon king.

▶ VISHNU *has ten different forms, or avatars. Some of these are shown here. (1) Matsya the fish* (see MANU); *(2) Narasimha, the man-lion; (3)* KRISHNA; *(4) Parasurama, who battles with the hundred-armed king of the Himalayas; (5) Kalkin, with a white horse.* (See also page 109.)

Although Hindu myths are the chief Indian myths, Buddhism also began in India. Buddhism was founded by Siddhartha GAUTAMA, a prince who lived during the 500s B.C. Appalled at people's suffering, the prince withdrew from his world of privilege to seek a meaning to life and an end to pain. When, after six years of meditation, he believed he had found the answers to these

questions, he became known as the Buddha—the "enlightened one." His teachings spread across India and Asia. In India, Buddhism was absorbed into Hindu beliefs; the Buddha was said to be a form of Vishnu.

Aditya is the mother of the Adityas, the gods of the months of the year. These are Ansa, Aryman, Bhaga, DAKSHA, Dhatri, Hitra, INDRA, Ravi, SAVITRI, SURYA, VARUNA, and YAMA.

▼ *The gods set out to produce* AMRITA *by churning the Ocean of Milk. First appeared Surabhi, the cow, which could grant any wish. Then Varuni, goddess of wine, appeared and Parijata, the tree of Paradise, which perfumed the world with its flowers. Next came the Moon, and* LAKSHMI, *goddess of plenty. Finally, the amrita was produced.*

ADITYA A mother goddess. In the *Vedas* she is married to VISHNU, but when he later appears on Earth as the dwarf Vamana, one of Vishnu's incarnations or avatars, she is said to be his mother.

■

AGNI The god of fire and one of the three chief gods in the *Vedas* (the other two are INDRA and SURYA). He is the god both of the fire of sacrifice and the household fire needed for cooking and warmth. One episode in the *Mahabharata* tells how Agni exhausted his strength by eating too many of the offerings people had made to him. To renew his power, he was obliged to burn down a forest. Agni is also the god of marriage: a newlywed couple walks around a fire seven times to bless their union.

AMRITA The water of eternal life, which the gods set out to obtain by churning the Ocean of Milk. With the help of the demons, they used a mountain to churn the milk by winding a thousand-headed serpent around it and pulling first one way, then the other. To help them, VISHNU took the form of a turtle to act as a pivot on which the mountain could turn. He also sat unseen on top of the mountain, thereby supporting the gods with his energy. Finally, the amrita was produced.

At this point the demons seized the amrita. If they had drunk it, they would have become indestructible and far more powerful than the gods. Vishnu, however, turned himself into a beautiful woman, for whose favor the demons began fighting among themselves. While they argued, he took the amrita and gave it to the gods.

■

ARJUNA A commander of the Pandawa family, whose war against the Korawas is at the center of the epic poem the *Mahabharata*. The *Bhagavad-Gita*, one of the major sacred Hindu works, appears in the *Mahabharata* as a pre-battle conversation between Arjuna and his chariot driver, KRISHNA.

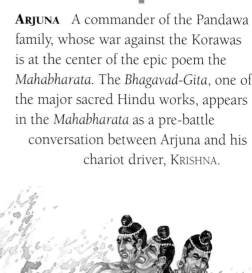

BALARAMA The fair-skinned brother of KRISHNA. It is said that VISHNU took two hairs, one white and one black, and planted them in the bodies of two different women. These became Balarama and Krishna. The brothers grew up together and shared many adventures.

BHARATA The half-brother of Prince RAMA, the hero of the *Ramayana*. When Rama was sent into exile, Bharata would not rule in his place, but went to the forest to beg his brother to return. When Rama refused, Bharata ruled in his name for 14 years and gave up the throne at once when the prince finally returned.

BRAHMA The first god of the sacred Hindu trinity, or trimurti, that also includes SHIVA and VISHNU. He is the creator of the universe, who in one story is said to have been born from a golden egg that floated on the first waters. Brahma has four faces, is usually gold or red in color, and wears a white robe.

BUDDHA *see* **GAUTAMA BUDDHA**

DAKSHA The son of BRAHMA, who sprang from the god's left thumb. One story tells how he invited all the gods except SHIVA to a sacrifice. To avenge the insult, Shiva appeared anyway and tore off Daksha's head, flinging it into the sacrificial fire. Shiva later calmed down and gave Daksha a goat's head to replace his own.

DEVI An important mother goddess who has many incarnations, some gentle and some fearsome. She appears in different forms, often as SHIVA's wife. At first, several goddesses were recognized as Shiva's wife, but these eventually unified as Devi. (*See also* DURGA, KALI, PARVATI.)

DURGA A warrior goddess and one of the avatars of DEVI. Durga is invincible in battle and was created by the gods to destroy a buffalo monster that was threatening their power. Taking a weapon in each of her ten hands, she killed the beast.

GANESHA The elephant-headed god of wisdom and a son of SHIVA and PARVATI. In one myth, his proud mother asked Saturn to look upon her son. A glance from the planet reduced her child's head to ashes. BRAHMA told Parvati to replace her son's head with the first that she could find, and this was an elephant's head.

GARUDA A fantastic creature, half man and half eagle, on which VISHNU rides. In some stories he is said to be the Sun in the form of a bird. He is king of the birds and the devourer of serpents and all evil things.

▲ GARUDA, *the fabulous and radiant king of the birds, carries Vishnu and his wife Lakshmi across the sky.*

BHARATA's great loyalty inspired the Hindu name for India—Bharata-Varsha—which means the "country of Bharata."

The city of Calcutta is named after the terrifying goddess KALI. It is known as Kali-ghat, meaning "Kali's steps."

▼ *A giant fish warned Vaivaswata, one of the* MANU, *that a flood was about to destroy the world. It told Vaivaswata to build a boat and to stock it with seeds and animals. As the waters rose, Vaivaswata fastened a rope to a horn on the fish, which towed the boat safely through the waves until the waters went down.*

GAUTAMA BUDDHA   A prince from northern India who was born in 563 B.C. He lived his early years in luxury, but at the age of 29 he realized that there was terrible suffering beyond the walls of his home. He decided to leave his riches and go in search of enlightenment—this meant understanding why human suffering existed and how it might be prevented. After many years of wandering he sat to meditate under a bodhi tree, and it was here he achieved understanding. He became the Buddha and spent the rest of his life preaching what he had learned.

■

HANUMAN   The son of the wind god and a monkey hero in the *Ramayana*. When RAMA's wife, SITA, was kidnapped by the demon RAVANA, Hanuman was sent to rescue her. Ravana captured him and set his tail on fire, but the monkey escaped and set fire to Ravana's kingdom with his burning tail. He later returned with Rama and the monkey army to defeat Ravana.

INDRA   The king of the gods in the *Vedas*, an early collection of Hindu hymns. Indra was also the god of battle, storms, and the Sun. He is usually shown as a four-armed figure, armed with his thunderbolt, and riding on a white elephant. He does not take such a major role in later Hinduism.

■

KALI   The most terrible aspect of DEVI. She was sent to Earth to destroy a race of demons but caused such devastation that countless people died. To bring an end to the slaughter, her husband, SHIVA, threw himself upon the dead bodies. Only when Kali realized that she was trampling on Shiva's corpse did she come to her senses. She has four hands—one holds a sword, another a severed head, both symbols of death; the other hands hold a holy book and prayer beads, both symbols of life.

■

KARTTIKEYA   The six-headed, six-armed war god and a son of SHIVA and PARVATI. He became a great warrior who conquered and slew the demon giant Taraka and restored peace to Heaven and Earth.

■

KRISHNA   The eighth avatar of VISHNU and a very popular figure. He appears in the *Mahabharata*. A section of this epic poem is known as the *Bhagavad-Gita* and is an extremely important and sacred Hindu text. It is a pre-battle conversation between ARJUNA, an army commander, and Krishna, who is disguised as his chariot driver. Krishna reveals his true identity and teaches that salvation is found through devotion to Vishnu.

■

LAKSHMI   The wife of VISHNU and goddess of abundance, good luck, and beauty. According to one legend, she rose from the froth during the churning of the Ocean of Milk.   (*See also* AMRITA.)

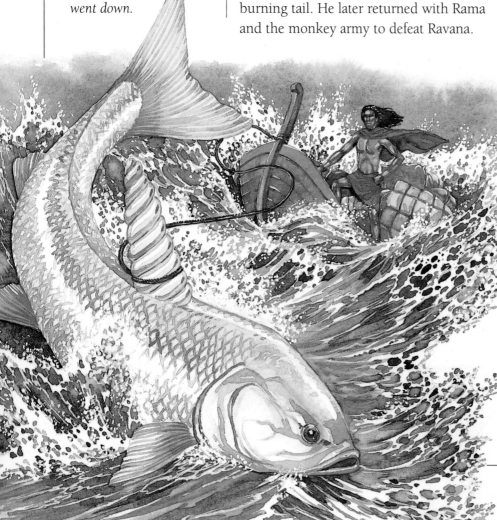

MANU The group name of 14 legendary beings who were the ancestors of all humankind. The seventh Manu, called Vaivaswata, once rescued a tiny fish, which is said to be Matsya, an avatar of VISHNU. Vaivaswata cared for the fish until it grew to an enormous size and had to be released into the ocean. The fish later came back to Vaivaswata and told him to build a boat because a huge flood was coming. All living things were destroyed in the deluge, except Vaivaswata who was kept safe in his boat. He offered a sacrifice so that he might be given a wife, and this wish was granted by the gods. The children of the marriage were the first generation of Manu, the Hindus of today.

MARUTS Storm gods and warrior companions of INDRA. They are the sons of the goddess Diti. When she was pregnant, her unborn baby was shattered into many pieces by a thunderbolt thrown by Indra. From the pieces, the 60 (or, in some accounts, 27) Maruts were born.

NANDIN A sacred white bull, on which SHIVA travels. In some accounts he is said to have once been a man of great wisdom who later achieved holy status. An image of him is often found guarding the entrance to temples dedicated to Shiva.

PARVATI An aspect of DEVI, whose name means "mountain girl." She is the daughter of the Himalayas. She was in love with SHIVA, but he took no notice of her and she withdrew to a mountain to practice meditation. One day a brahman (a Hindu holy man) visited her and asked why she hid from the world. She told him it was because she desired only Shiva. The brahman then revealed himself to be Shiva in disguise and the two were married.

PUSHAN A god known as the Prosperor. He guards roads, protects cattle, and guides travelers on their journey. He once went to a ceremony given by DAKSHA, where SHIVA knocked out his teeth in a rage. Since then, he has become known as the "toothless god," and has to eat gruel. He is often shown in a cart pulled by goats.

RAMA An avatar, or incarnation, of VISHNU, and the hero prince of the *Ramayana*. He was the elder son of King Dasaratha of Ayodya and was sent into exile because of his stepmother's plotting. While in exile he fought a great battle against the powers of evil, which were led by RAVANA, king of the demons. Ravana had kidnapped Rama's wife, SITA, and the prince rescued her and defeated the demon forces with the help of HANUMAN, the monkey king. Rama then reigned as king on Earth, before entering Heaven.

▲ *The war god* KARTTIKEYA *was also known as Skanda. He was the son of* SHIVA, *but there are different stories concerning the identity of his mother. In one story his mother is said to be* PARVATI, *but in another he is said to be the son of six star goddesses. As a war god, Karttikeya was shown holding a spear or bow and arrow, and riding a peacock.*

▲ SARASVATI is *the beautiful wife of* BRAHMA. *She rides a white swan and plays a stringed musical instrument called a vina. She is associated with water, and her name may have come from the sacred river Sarasvati in Rajastan.*

RAVANA   The ten-headed king of the Rakshasas, hideous demons and evil spirits. Their name means "harmers." Ravana had 10 heads, 20 arms, and a body as large as a mountain. He was covered in scars from battles with the gods, but he could only be killed by a mortal. Ravana caused such havoc that VISHNU adopted human form and came to Earth as RAMA. The story is told in the *Ramayana*. Ravana abducted Rama's wife, SITA, and took her away to his island kingdom of Lanka. Rama fought against him, but every time he cut off one of the demon's heads, another grew back in its place. Finally, Rama fired a sacred arrow at Ravana's heart. The demon king fell down dead, and the great battle was won.

RIBHUS   A group of mortal craftsmen who were raised to the rank of gods after they built a golden chariot for INDRA. They now live close to the Sun and hold up the sky.

SARASVATI   The goddess of wisdom, learning, music, and the arts. She is said to have invented Sanskrit, the language of the Hindus. Sarasvati is also the wife of BRAHMA and was so beautiful that her husband grew three more faces so that he could see her on every side of him.

SATI   The loyal wife of SHIVA, and one of the incarnations, or avatars, of the goddess DEVI. When all the gods except Shiva were invited by DAKSHA to a special ceremony, Sati was so ashamed on her husband's behalf that she sacrificed herself in the fire. The goddess PARVATI, who also wed Shiva, is said to be a reincarnation of Sati.

SAVITRI   A heroine in the *Mahabharata* who restored her dead husband, Satyavan, to life by persuading YAMA, the god of death, to release him.

Savitri is also the name of the deity of the rising and setting Sun in the *Vedas*.

SHIVA   One of the three great Hindu gods of the trimurti (the other two are BRAHMA and VISHNU). Shiva is called the Destroyer, but his enormous destructive powers have a positive purpose because they create the conditions for renewal. He is often shown with a third eye that, depending on his mood, can illuminate or destroy anything taken in by its fiery glance. When the gods were churning the Ocean of Milk to produce AMRITA, the serpent that they used to turn the mountain became so exhausted that it spat out venom. The poison threatened to engulf and destroy the Earth, so Vishnu sent for Shiva. He swallowed the venom, which changed the color of his throat to blue.

In one of his many forms, Shiva haunts cemeteries, where he strings together the skulls of the dead to make a grim garland.

SITA The wife of RAMA in the *Ramayana*, said to be an incarnation, or avatar, of LAKSHMI. She was kidnapped by RAVANA, the demon king, and taken to his kingdom of Lanka. Rama rescued her but doubted that she had been faithful to him while in captivity. To prove her innocence, Sita jumped into a fire. The fire god AGNI then rose from the flames with Sita unharmed on his lap and reunited her with Rama.

SURYA The Sun god and the ruler of the sky. He is one of an ancient trinity of gods, the others being AGNI (ruler of the Earth) and INDRA (ruler of the air). Surya rides in a chariot drawn by seven horses driven by Aruna ("the dawn"). His heat is so intense that his wife fled into a forest to keep cool, leaving behind Shade to be his mistress.

USHAS The goddess of dawn in the *Vedas*. She is a beautiful young woman who is sometimes seen as a contented wife pleased to look after the home. But she is also said to represent the inevitability of death.

VARUNA A sky god and one of the most important gods in the *Vedas*. He was the possessor of all knowledge since he had a thousand eyes that could see all things. He made paths for the Sun, the stars, and rivers; he controlled the winds, sent refreshing rain, and gave fire to humankind. Varuna upheld justice, and his unlimited powers made him the guardian of the universe.

VISHNU One of the three great Hindu gods in the trimurti (the other two are BRAHMA and SHIVA). He has a good and merciful nature and is known as the Protector. When humankind is in peril, Vishnu descends to Earth and resolves the crisis by adopting one of his incarnations, or avatars. These take the form of a human hero or a supernatural animal. Two of the most popular of his avatars are KRISHNA and RAMA.

YAMA The god of death. He visits people at their appointed hour and takes their souls away for judgment.

YUGA A unit of time known as an age of the world in the Hindu universe. There are four yugas that form a cycle known as a mahayuga, which lasts for 4,320,000 years. Two thousand mahayugas make a kalpa, which is one day in BRAHMA's life.

◄ SHIVA *in the form of Nataraja, the Lord of the Dance. His dancing represents the eternal movement of the universe. A demon dwarf is trampled, symbolizing Shiva's power to destroy.*

VISHNU has appeared as nine different avatars so far.
- As Matsya, the fish, he saved one of the MANU from a great flood.
- As Kurma, the turtle, he helped the other gods produce AMRITA.
- As Varaha, the boar, he battled for a thousand years against a giant.
- As Narasimha, the man-lion, he killed the giant's tyrannical brother.
- As Vamana, the dwarf, he won back the Earth and Heaven for the gods after they had been taken by the king of the giants.
- As Parasurama, he killed the hundred-armed king of the Himalayas.
- Vishnu's seventh and eighth avatars are the extremely popular RAMA and KRISHNA.
- The Hindu priests claim that Vishnu's ninth avatar is the BUDDHA.
- Kalkin, the future avatar, will appear on a white horse and destroy the wicked forever.

· CHINA ·

The Chinese have some of the oldest myths and legends in the world, with some myths dating back nearly 4,000 years. Many of these first stories are concerned with creation, tales of the ancient rulers, and the fight between good and evil. There is a preoccupation with magic, ghosts, the dead, and the supernatural. During the time when the Shang dynasty ruled China (c. 1600–1066 B.C.), the people worshiped many different gods. These symbolized various elements of nature, such as the Earth, the rain, or the rivers. Their supreme god was SHANG DI. People asked the advice of ancestor spirits by scratching questions on pieces of bone or turtle shell. These were heated up and the marks changed shape. The new markings were read as messages from the ancestors.

The Zhou dynasty (1066–221 B.C.) followed the Shang dynasty. During this time, ancestor worship became widespread, but some people continued to worship the old gods.

Between 500 B.C. and 400 B.C., two schools of thought grew popular. These were Daoism (which is often spelled Taoism) and Confucianism. Both had a great effect on Chinese beliefs and are two of the three main traditional Chinese religions. (Buddhism, which arrived in China later from India, is the third).

▶ *A Chinese myth tells how ten suns once appeared together in the sky. Rocks melted and plants withered. The archer* YI *saved the Earth by shooting nine of the suns down.*

The Chinese believe in two opposite forces called Yin and Yang. Yin is the female principle; Yang, the male. In the Daoist image of Yin and Yang shown here, Yin is dark, and Yang light. The two came together to form the first being, a giant called PAN KU, who began to create the universe from his body.

Confucianism and Daoism

The new teachings were designed to offer people a code to live their life by. At first they did not involve myths and supernatural beings, but through time myths grew up around them.

CONFUCIUS taught about the importance of social order and stressed that people should respect their parents, the old, the dead, and the ways of the past. Daoism is based on the philosophy of LAO ZI, and developed into a religion between 100 B.C. and 200 B.C.

Daoists believe that the way to attain eternal life is through understanding the natural laws, living in harmony with nature, and, especially, balancing the opposing principles of Yin and Yang. The Daoists adopted aspects of Chinese folk religion and came to believe in many different, protective gods.

Confucius never talked about life after death, and when Buddhism was brought to China between 50 B.C. and A.D. 50, it answered many questions about the next world.

Chinese myths were passed on both orally and in written texts. China has a great tradition of literature and scholarship. Anyone could rise through society by passing examinations which showed that they had learned certain classic texts by heart.

Buddhism states that after people die they will be born again or, if they lead very moral and exemplary lives, they could become buddhas and live in Paradise. Buddhism had a great impact on Chinese mythology. GUAN YIN, the goddess of mercy, and the most important goddess to the Chinese people, is of Buddhist origin.

Chinese society had a rigid pyramid structure, with the emperor at the top. In Chinese myths, Heaven and Hell are structured in a similar way. There was a mythical king in charge of Hell, with ten judges and courts of Hell below him. A mythical emperor—known as the JADE EMPEROR—was in charge of Heaven and also presided over the courts, judges, and officials. On Earth, the emperor was called the "Son of Heaven" to show that he was connected with the hierarchies of Heaven.

▲ In Chinese mythology, human beings can become gods after their death. The Men Shen, or "Door Gods," are one example. They were generals in the army of an emperor of the Tang dynasty, who was haunted in his sleep by demons around his bed. The generals stood guard at his door to protect him, and the demons never returned. The generals were later made into gods. Other humans who became gods include the AZURE DRAGON, GUAN DI, WEN CHANG, and ZHONG KWEI.

AZURE DRAGON Dragons have always been important in Chinese mythology. The emperor was called a dragon, and dragons often decorate the walls of Chinese temples. The Azure Dragon embodies the spirit of the hero Teng Qing Gong, a great general at the beginning of the 1300s. During his life, Teng Qing Gong overcame mighty supernatural powers. He broke his left arm while fighting NE ZHA and was captured and executed. The title Azure Dragon was given to him many years later.

BA SIN The "Eight Immortals," legendary figures from Daoist beliefs. They lived at different times and had great powers, such as the ability to walk across water. Each represents a different condition in life: masculinity, femininity, age, youth, poverty, wealth, nobility, and commonness.

BEI DI The "Northern Emperor." A legendary hero in Daoist mythology who subdued a monster that was ravaging the world. Because of his miraculous deeds he was rewarded with eternal life and made into the First Lord of Heaven.

CHENG HUANG The "City Gods." The name given to local gods who protect and administer each town or district. They are loyal figures who report back to the JADE EMPEROR and are known for their efficiency and good deeds.

CHI GUNG A monk known as the "living Buddha." His clothing was always torn and he drank too much, but he was very wise, kind, and performed many miracles.

CONFUCIUS One of the most important Chinese philosophers, he lived in the 400s B.C. He preached a code of ethical behavior for public and private life. He worked as a local official and once tested the moral integrity of the district prince by sending him a troupe of dancing girls. They so distracted the prince from his work that Confucius left in disgust to find a more moral governor.

DOU MOU The Daoist goddess of the North Star who had nine children, known as the Jen Huang. These were the first human rulers of the world. Dou Mou lives in Heaven in a palace with her husband. Her sons have their own palace nearby.

EIGHT IMMORTALS *see* **BA SIN**

GUAN DI The god of war and patron of literature. He was born as a mortal in the A.D. 100s, but became so famous as a heroic warrior that he was later honored as a god. He is usually shown with a red face, which is explained in a well-known story. An evil town official captured a young woman to keep as his mistress. Guan Di killed the official and rescued the woman. When he hid in a temple to avoid capture, soldiers set fire to the building, forcing him to leap out and kill them all. But the flames had turned his face bright red, and he was able to escape from the town unrecognized.

GUAN YIN The goddess of mercy and patron of children. She has many forms, some male and others female. In one story, Guan Yin was the saintly daughter of an evil ruler during the Zhou dynasty. She wished to become a Buddhist nun, but her father refused her and had her killed. Guan Yin's soul went down to the Underworld. Her purity transformed that grim realm into a paradise. The gods of the Underworld were so alarmed that they asked the Buddha to take her away, and he restored her to life.

Before long, her father was struck blind with the plague. Guan Yin gave up her eyes in order that he might see. He was so moved by her selfless act that he became a good man, and his act of conversion made Guan Yin whole again.

JADE EMPEROR The supreme god of Daoism and the king of Heaven. His real name is Yu Huang, or the "August Personage of Jade." He rules over a vast system of divine offices, each administered by a less important god. In Heaven, the Jade Emperor held a similar position to the Chinese emperor on Earth.

KITCHEN GOD *see* **TSAO WANG**

KSHITIGARBHA BODHISATTVA The guardian of the Earth who has power over the ten courts of Hell (*see page 111*). A bodhisattva is an enlightened being who returns to the Earth to help the needy and suffering. Kshitigarbha is a compassionate bodhisattva, who led all the suffering souls from the Underworld to Heaven.

LAO ZI A philosopher in the 400s B.C. who founded Daoism. He lived around the same time as CONFUCIUS, and the two men are said to have once met. Lao Zi preached that people should practice simple lives in harmony with nature, and his beliefs are collected in a book known as the *Dao De Ching*, or "book of the way."

His mother was said to have been made pregnant by a falling star, and then to have carried Lao Zi inside her for 81 years. Eventually, she gave birth to a white-haired baby who could already speak. For 160 years he lived as a hermit and preached, before making a journey to the west; he was never heard from again.

▼ *The* JADE EMPEROR *became the supreme Daoist god after one of the Song dynasty emperors claimed to be in direct contact with him. The Jade Emperor lives in a palace in Heaven, where he establishes order by creating an organization very like a system of government offices. Though he is in charge, he has become too important to deal with matters himself. All the work is done by the lesser gods.*

▲ LUNG MO, *known as the "Dragon Mother," seated on the back of the dragon that she had raised from the moment it hatched from its egg.*

The White Tiger of the West is a demon killer who attacks evil and fends it off. He was once a man called Xin Cheng Xing, the son of a courtier, who died as he tried to avenge his father's death. His spirit became the White Tiger.

LUNG MO   The "Dragon Mother." She was an old woman who came across an egg and took it home. From the egg hatched a strange creature, which in time she realized was a dragon. The two lived together, and the dragon brought her good luck. One day the emperor ordered Lung Mo to attend his court and explain how she dared raise such an imperial creature. As she walked to the palace, Lung Mo began to feel homesick, so the dragon took her home on its back. After her death she was honored as a goddess, for no one else had ever been carried by a dragon.

MONKEY   Also called the "great sage, equal of Heaven." He was born from a stone egg at the top of the Mountain of Fruit and Flowers. He became king of the monkeys, but grew dissatisfied since he wanted to know how to live forever. A Daoist master taught him the way of eternal life, and Monkey then went up to Heaven, where he stole the peaches of immortality and generally behaved very badly. He only escaped punishment when GUAN YIN spoke on his behalf. Instead, he was entrusted to look after the priest Xuan Zang on his journey west to pick up the Buddhist scriptures.

NE ZHA   The son of a general called Li Zheng. He was born with a sash of red silk around his waist and a magic bracelet on his right wrist, which enabled him to perform many miraculous and heroic deeds. When he accidentally killed the son of the dragon king, Li Zheng was held responsible. To save his father from certain death, Ne Zha surrendered to the dragon king and paid for his crime by scraping the flesh off his own bones.

NU WA   The creator goddess, who came to live on Earth. She had the head and body of a beautiful woman, but from the waist down she was shaped like a serpent. She created humankind from river clay. A few she made herself, but most were made from spray as she whirled a vine around that had been dipped into the wet mud.

PAN KU   The creator of the universe. At the beginning of time the only thing that existed was a huge egg that contained chaos and the giant Pan Ku. When the giant broke out of the egg, chaos escaped and the lighter, purer parts (Yang) rose to become the sky, while the heavier, impure parts (Yin) sank to become the Earth. Pan Ku kept the two forces apart with his body, which grew almost ten feet (3 meters) a day for 18,000 years. At the end of that time the sky was secure above the Earth, and the giant died. From his body were made the Sun, Moon, and stars.

PI KAN   A god of wealth, who as a mortal was renowned for his wisdom. He was a relative of the evil emperor Chou Hsin but spoke out against the tyrant's cruelty. The emperor had heard that the heart of a wise man had seven holes, and so furious was he with Pi Kan's criticism that he had him cut open to see if it was true.

SAKYAMUNI The Buddha's real name. He is worshiped all over China but, in fact, he was a prince from India. (*See page 106.*)

SHANG DI A supreme sky god, said to be the ancestor of a Shang emperor who ruled China between 1700 B.C. and 1000 B.C. He is believed to have evolved into the Daoist JADE EMPEROR.

TIEN HOU When still a young girl, Tien Hou dreamed that her father's boat had capsized and that she had turned herself into a spirit to save him. She was able to calm a storm simply by closing her eyes. Tien Hou was later honored as the Imperial Concubine Queen of Heaven, and is now mainly revered by the fishermen in southern China.

TSAO WANG The kitchen god—a spirit who lives above the hearth. From there he watches the behavior of the household, and at the end of the year he reports to the JADE EMPEROR. Just before he is due to leave for Heaven, the family may spread honey on the lips of an image of Tsao Wang, so he will say only sweet words.

WEN CHANG A Daoist god of literature. As a mortal, he lived in Sichuan province during the Tang dynasty. He is often shown with a carp, which indicates good luck in examinations for public office.

YEN LO WONG The king of Hell. The Underworld was divided into ten hells, each headed by its own king. Yen Lo Wong examined the register that recorded all human deeds and sent the souls of the dead to one of these hells according to how badly they had behaved when alive.

YI An immortal archer hero who saved the Earth from being burned to cinders. In ancient times there were ten suns that took turns to come out each day. They grew tired of this routine and decided they would all come out at the same time. Before long, the plants began to wither and the rocks to melt. The emperor, Yao, begged Dijun, the father of the suns, to control his fiery children. But the suns would not listen. So Dijun sent Yi to Earth armed with a magic bow and arrows. Though he was meant only to frighten the mischievous suns into behaving, Yi shot nine of them out of the sky with his arrows, leaving only the Sun we see today. Dijun was so angry at the death of nine of his children that he banished the hero to Earth, to live as an ordinary mortal.

ZHONG KWEI A killer of demons and a ghost eater whose fearful image is placed on walls to keep away evil spirits. He was said to be able to tear ghosts apart with his teeth and swallow them whole. Zhong Kwei was a physician who lived during the Tang dynasty and who was rejected from the official national examinations because his face was so ugly. In despair, he committed suicide by drowning himself in the river.

▼ *When NU WA came down to live on Earth she became very lonely. One day as she was sitting by a river, she began to toy with the wet clay. She formed the shapes of men and women and breathed life into them. These became the rich people. She created poor people from spray that came off a vine as she whirled it around.*

·JAPAN·

The oldest religion of Japan is Shinto—a word that means "the way of the gods." Since the ancient Japanese did not have writing, nobody knows for certain when or how Shinto began. Confucianism was introduced to Japan in the A.D. 200s and Buddhism in the A.D. 500s. Both of these faiths influenced Shinto, so it is difficult to separate purely Japanese ideas from those brought from China.

The main written source of Japanese myths was completed in the A.D. 700s, and based on spoken myths. It is called the *Kojiki,* or "Records of Ancient Matters," and tells the story of the creation of the world and the myth of the original couple, IZANAGI AND IZANAMI. Another source is the *Nihongi,* or "Chronicles of Japan."

▶ *In the beginning, the Earth was not fully formed. IZANAGI AND IZANAMI stood on the Floating Bridge of Heaven and stirred the waters below them with a spear. A drop of water fell from the tip of the spear and formed an island, Onogoro. This was the first solid land.*

Izanagi and Izanami had several children, including the Sun goddess AMATERASU. She is the most important of all the Shinto deities: ten million people visit her sacred shrine at Ise every year. Traditionally, the royal family in Japan can claim that they are descendants of NINIGI, one of Amaterasu's grandchildren. (The Japanese emperor was seen as a human god until 1946, when he denied he was divine.) Because of this connection with the Sun goddess, the Rising Sun appears on the Japanese national flag.

Kami

The Japanese deities or spirits are called "kami"—a word used for all natural objects with awe-inspiring, sacred power, such as mountains, tall and ancient trees, rivers, and oceans, as well as powerful human beings. Traditionally, there are millions of kami. The kami are divided into gods of Heaven and gods of Earth, who live on islands in Japan. Earth and Heaven were at one time linked by a bridge and the gods moved between them until the bridge collapsed into the sea.

Buddhism came to Japan from China and has existed side by side with Shinto beliefs for around 1,500 years. The two faiths have had a great influence on each other. At one time, some Buddhist temples contained Shinto shrines, and Buddhist monks carried out the services at Shinto shrines. Buddhist ceremonies were used for funerals and at services to honor the dead. This was called Ryobu Shinto and explains why some Shinto gods are also figures in Buddhist mythology.

▲ *This clay figure was made between* A.D. *700 and* A.D. *800 and is over six feet (2 meters) high. It shows a ferocious god dressed as a warrior. The statue was placed in a holy building and was designed to protect the building from demons of the Underworld.*

▲ *At one time, the Sun goddess* AMATERASU *hid in a cave, taking light away from the world. At first she would not come out, but in the end, the dancing of another goddess persuaded her to peek from the cave.*

Mount Fuji is a dormant volcano that has been the most sacred mountain in Japan since ancient times. The mountain's spirit was said to protect the nation, and up until as late as the 1800s women were not allowed to climb it.

▲ BISHAMON *is usually portrayed as a warrior, carrying a spear and a miniature pagoda (a symbol of Buddhism).* DAIKOKU *stands on a mound of rice, carrying the hammer of wealth and accompanied by a rat, which protects him and uses holly to drive evil away.* HOTEI *usually appears as a fat Buddhist priest, carrying a bag of precious things.*

AMATERASU   The Sun goddess in Shinto mythology. She is believed to be the ancestor of the emperor and the founder of the royal house of Japan. She was born from the left eye of IZANAGI and had eight children from a marriage with her brother SUSANOWO. When her brother-husband treated her badly, she shut herself in the "cave of the heavens," and the world fell into darkness. Nothing would persuade her to come out until Uzume, the goddess of laughter, began an exotic dance in front of the cave. Out of curiosity, Amaterasu sneaked a look and noticed a mirror and a string of jewels placed on a tree by other gods. The goddess was so fascinated by her reflection that she came out of the cave, and light returned to the world.

BATO KANNON   One of seven different forms of KANNON in Buddhist myth. He is shown wearing a horse's head as a crown, and has a third eye and a fanged mouth. He is the guardian of all those who have been reborn as an animal as a result of their deeds in their previous life.

■

BENTEN   The goddess of the sea, and one of the seven gods of good fortune. She is mainly worshiped on the outlying Japanese islands.   (*See* SHICHI FUKUJIN.)

■

BINZUKI   A disciple of the Buddha who was raised to the rank of a god because he had miraculous powers of healing.

■

BISHAMON   A war god, usually shown wearing armor. He is one of the seven gods of good fortune.   (*See* SHICHI FUKUJIN.)

■

DAIKOKU   The very popular god of wealth, prosperity, and happiness, and one of the seven gods of good fortune. He can make a person rich with a single stroke of his wooden hammer.   (*See* SHICHI FUKUJIN.)

EBISU The god of work, often shown holding a fishing rod. He is one of the gods of good fortune. (*See* SHICHI FUKUJIN.)

EMMA-O The Buddhist god of the Underworld, whose realm is divided into eight hells of fire and eight of ice. He sits in judgment over the souls of dead men and sends them to the hell most fitting to their sins. Women are judged by his sister.

FUKUROKUJU The god of wisdom and long life, and one of the seven gods of good fortune. (*See* SHICHI FUKUJIN.)

HACHIMAN A Shinto war god. Originally, he was the Emperor Ojin (A.D. 270–310), who was honored as a god when he died. Later still, he became identified with the gentle Buddhist god KANNON.

HOTEI The god of happiness, known as the laughing Buddha, and one of the gods of good fortune. (*See* SHICHI FUKUJIN.)

INARI The god of agriculture, rice, and prosperity. He is said to live in the hills, and the fox, which is sacred to him, acts as his messenger. Two red-painted foxes usually flank his image at all Inari shrines.

IZANAGI AND IZANAMI Shinto creator gods. They formed the Japanese islands by stirring the waters of chaos with a jeweled spear. Izanami died giving birth to their son KAGUTSUCHI. Izanagi searched in the Underworld for his wife, but found her rotting body and fled in horror. On reaching the upper world he cleansed himself in a river. Gods and evil creatures were born from his discarded clothes. As he washed his face, AMATERASU was born from his left eye, TSUKI YOMI from his right eye, and SUSANOWO from his nose.

JIZO The Buddhist protector of all who suffer pain. He is known as the great guardian of children, especially the souls of those who have died. Jizo can save souls from Hell and take them to Paradise.

JOROJIN The god of long life and wisdom. He is one of the seven gods of good fortune. (*See* SHICHI FUKUJIN.)

KAGUTSUCHI The Shinto fire god and the fourth son of IZANAGI AND IZANAMI. His mother was so badly burned giving birth to him that she died. In a fit of rage, Izanagi cut his newborn son into pieces.

KANNON An important Buddhist deity who appears as both a male and a female figure. Kannon is a compassionate being and the patron of children, women in childbirth, and dead souls. Kannon has many different aspects. (*See* BATO KANNON.)

Mount Fuji, the extinct volcano near Tokyo, takes its name from Fuchi. She was the fire goddess of the Ainu, the first people who lived in Japan.

▲ *A sword guard dating from the 1800s, engraved with the figure of* KANNON *riding on the back of a carp. Kannon was a popular bodhisattva (Buddha-to-be) and took many forms. This merciful figure was worshiped by sailors to protect them against shipwreck.*

RAIDEN likes nothing more than a young belly to feast on. Children are warned to keep their stomachs covered, so as not to tempt his awful appetite.

The magic objects that the SHICHI FUKUJIN carried in their treasure ship included a hat of invisibility, a lucky rain hat, keys to the divine treasure house, a change purse that never empties, a cloak of feathers, rolls of silk, and scrolls or books.

NINIGI The grandson of the Shinto goddess AMATERASU. When O KUNI NUSHI became ruler of the province of Izumo, his brothers waged war against him constantly, and the land fell into chaos. Amaterasu forced O Kuni Nushi to give up the throne in favor of her grandson. Ninigi brought with him to Earth the jewels and mirror that were used to tempt Amaterasu out of hiding, and the Kusanagi sword that SUSANOWO had pulled from the dragon's tail. These are the symbols of imperial power in Japan. Ninigi was told to honor the mirror as if it were Amaterasu herself. He married SENGEN, and the royal family of Japan are said to be their descendants.

▼ *The* SHICHI FUKUJIN *include* JOROJIN, *the god of long life. He is usually shown as an old man, often accompanied by a crane that symbolizes contented old age. In his hand he holds a scroll containing the world's wisdom.*

O KUNI NUSHI The Shinto god of medicine, who invented cures for many diseases. He had 80 brothers who were jealous of his powers and tried to destroy him. He was saved by his mother, who sent him to the Underworld to seek the protection of SUSANOWO. There he met Susanowo's daughter, Suseri Hime. They fell in love and married. This so outraged Susanowo that he tried to kill O Kuni Nushi by first putting snakes and then poisonous insects into the room where he slept. Each time, O Kuni Nushi was saved by a magic scarf given to him by his bride. In the end, the couple escaped to Earth, where O Kuni Nushi became ruler of the province of Izumo. The realm was reduced to chaos because his brothers kept attacking him, forcing AMATERASU to step in and make O Kuni Nushi abdicate.

■

RAIDEN A thunder god, often portrayed as a red demon with horns on his head and two claws on each foot. He beats a set of drums to make the sound of thunder.

■

SENGEN The Shinto goddess of Mount Fuji, who was also known as "the princess who makes the flowers of the tree blossom." She married NINIGI, and their great grandson, Jimmu Tennu, was the legendary first emperor of Japan.

■

SHICHI FUKUJIN The seven Shinto gods of good fortune. These are BENTEN, BISHAMON, DAIKOKU, EBISU, FUKUROKUJU, HOTEI, and JOROJIN. They are a popular subject of folk songs. They can be seen alone, or together on their treasure ship, which contains the magic objects that implement their powers.

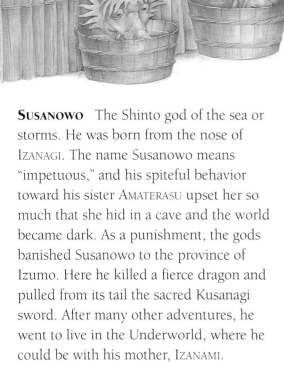

SUSANOWO The Shinto god of the sea or storms. He was born from the nose of IZANAGI. The name Susanowo means "impetuous," and his spiteful behavior toward his sister AMATERASU upset her so much that she hid in a cave and the world became dark. As a punishment, the gods banished Susanowo to the province of Izumo. Here he killed a fierce dragon and pulled from its tail the sacred Kusanagi sword. After many other adventures, he went to live in the Underworld, where he could be with his mother, IZANAMI.

■

TEMMANGU The god of learning and writing, and the patron of teachers and schoolchildren. He was born a mortal but became a god when he died.

■

TENGU Mischievous trickster spirits. They are half human, wearing hats and cloaks, and half bird, with wings, claws, and elongated beaks. Hence their name, which means "long nose."

TSUKI YOMI The Shinto Moon god, born from the right eye of IZANAGI. He climbed the Ladder of Heaven to live with his sister, the Sun goddess AMATERASU. She sent Tsuki Yomi as her representative to UKE MOCHI, the goddess of food. When Tsuki Yomi killed Uke Mochi, Amaterasu was so angry that she refused to see him ever again. From then on, the Moon god and the Sun goddess have lived apart, and time has been divided into day and night.

■

UKE MOCHI The Shinto goddess of food. When TSUKI YOMI went to see her, Uke Mochi invited him to stay for a meal and produced a feast of rice and other dishes from her mouth and nose. Tsuki Yomi was so disgusted at being offered a meal in such a manner that he killed the food goddess. From her dead body grew rice, corn, and beans; from her head came an ox and a horse. All these things AMATERASU gave to humankind for its own use.

In a later version of this story, Uke Mochi is killed by SUSANOWO.

▲ SUSANOWO *outwitted an eight-headed dragon that had devoured seven daughters of a grieving couple and was about to eat the eighth. Susanowo built a fence and placed along its length eight buckets of rice wine, each beneath a hatch. Sticking a head through each hatch, the dragon drank so much wine that it fell asleep. Susanowo cut off all the sleeping heads.*

·SOUTHEAST ASIA·

There are many islands that make up Southeast Asia, and a great variety of cultures. For thousands of years the area has been a main trade route in Asia. Different peoples have settled there and brought their beliefs with them. Islam and Buddhism are now the major religions, but Hindu beliefs were once very important throughout Southeast Asia. As evidence of this, the stories told in the Indian epic poems the *Ramayana* and *Mahabharata* are still popular on the islands of Bali and Java.

Alongside these major religions, ancient beliefs in ancestors, spirits, and mythical animals still exist. Many of these ancestors and spirits are venerated locally and may not be found on neighboring islands.

Ancestor spirits

In some Southeast Asian myths, a village is said to have been founded by a legendary ancestor. The ancestors may be heroes who reveal the rules of proper behavior to their people and teach them the skills they need to survive. Ancestors provide a link between the living and the dead, and rituals for the dead are an important part of community life.

◄ In Myanmar, the many types of spirits are called NATS. Some will cause trouble if offended.

▲ According to a Balinese myth, nothing existed before the World Serpent, Antaboga, created the World Turtle. On the turtle's back lie two coiled snakes and a black stone. This stone is the lid to the entrance to the Underworld.

In some communities, the spirits of ancestors are believed to protect people from evil and shrines or monuments are often built to them. The Toraja peoples on Sulawesi carve TAU TAU sculptures and place them in caves. Although the Toraja are now Christian, belief in the protection of ancestors still exists.

A myth in Borneo tells how, in the beginning, gods had homes in the heavens, while the Earth below them was only sea. The land was formed when gods threw rocks down from the sky to make the different islands of the world.

Spirits and fantastic beasts

The spirit world is important to the people of Southeast Asia. In Myanmar spirits are called NATS, which means "lord." This reflects the respect that these spirits receive. Nats are protectors, but can also be terrible if they are not properly revered.

Myths about fantastic beasts are widespread throughout the region. Animals that look like dragons or snakes are especially popular. In Sumatra, for example, the Underworld is said to be ruled by a serpent called NAGA PADOHA. *Naga* is an ancient Hindu word for snake, which suggests that these myths first came from India. Today, stories about nagas are common all over Southeast Asia.

The dragonlike monsters have different names, such as the ASO on Borneo, and SINGA on Sumatra. They are called on for protection, and may have come originally from China.

▲ *A group of Tau Tau carvings of dead ancestors, placed high in caves on the island of Sulawesi.*

Most of the people in Southeast Asia live in villages in the countryside. They make their living from growing rice, which is the staple food of the region. As a result, myths about rice are common and offerings are made to the gods and goddesses for a good harvest.

On Bali, families make figures called "rice mothers" out of one long sheaf of rice. They tie them to the edge of the fields where the rice is grown to make sure there is a good crop. After the harvest, the rice mother is blessed by a priest and placed in the family rice store to guard the crop.

On Laos, the Lamet peoples say that rice has a soul, and it is given the same name as the human soul: "klpu." People make many offerings to protect the soul of the rice because it is the power that makes the crop grow.

In Malayan mythology, demons, ghosts, and spirits are grouped together under the name "hantu." Hantu B'rok is a spirit who takes control of dancers. The Hantu Ayer and Hantu Laut are water spirits, and the Hantu Kubor are demons of the grave.

On Timor island, the creator god of the Tetum peoples is called Maromak. He is associated with the sky, and sacrifices and prayers are offered to him. He came down to Earth with a goddess called Rai Lolon, and together they made the first human beings. These people are said to have climbed from the craters that dot the local Timorese landscape.

NATS are part of a complex system of spirit worship. Among the most important is a group known as the "Thirty Seven Nats." These are the souls of legendary men and women whose lives came to a violent end. Nats are believed to be more powerful than humans, and many are mischievous, often unpredictable, and can even be dangerous.

ASO In Borneo, a dragonlike creature that protects people from evil spirits. Many objects are decorated with its image.

ATUF A hero of the Tanimbarese people from Indonesia. A long time ago, when the world was in darkness, Atuf brought light when he sailed to the eastern horizon and speared the Sun into pieces with his magic lance to create the Moon and stars.

HKUN AI In Myanmar, a mythical hero who married Naga, a dragon woman. Most of the time his wife took human shape, but during the dragon's Water Festival she reassumed her serpentlike body. Hkun Ai was so disturbed by his wife's changed shape that he decided he could no longer live with her. Before he went, Naga gave him an egg, which in time hatched to produce a baby boy. The child grew up to be a great king, Tung Hkan.

KADAKLAN In Philippine mythology, the creator god of the Tinguian islands. He beats on his drum to make thunder, while the bite of his dog is said to be lightning.

LAC LONG QUAN In the mythology of Vietnam, a dragon lord who taught people how to grow rice and wear clothes. He then left them, promising to return in a time of need. One day a Chinese ruler tried to conquer Vietnam, and the people cried out to Lac Long Quan. He returned as promised and drove the invader away.

MIN MAHAGIRI The household spirit, or NAT, in Myanmar. He was a powerful blacksmith during his life; however, the king had him killed. A coconut is hung on the porch of every home in his honor. He is portrayed holding a sword and a leaf fan.

MOYANG MELUR A spirit, half human and half tiger, in Malayan mythology. He lived on the Moon, where the rules of civilized behavior were kept. On Earth, human beings behaved like savages, because they did not know about the rules of society. One day, Moyang Melur was watching the chaos below when he leaned too far forward and fell to Earth. Unless he was returned at once he would have destroyed the human race. A hunter called Moyang Kapir threw a rope to the Moon and climbed there with the spirit.

▼ *While on the Moon, the hunter Moyang Kapir found a bag containing the rules of behavior, which* MOYANG MELUR *had hidden. The hunter escaped with the bag down a rope to Earth and gave the rules to his people.*

NAGA PADOHA   A giant dragon serpent that lives in the Underworld, according to the Indonesian people of Sumatra. It is often portrayed as a scaly-skinned buffalo, or as a huge serpent with horns.

■

NAT   In Myanmar, the name for a supernatural being. A nat may be both good and evil, and lives in the sea, the air, or on land. Nats are sometimes said to be the spirits of people who died violently.

■

PAWANG PUKAT   In Malayan mythology, a wizard who had terrible luck. In the end, he decided to improve his fortunes with magic. He carried a huge quantity of leaves out to sea, scattered them around with handfuls of yellow rice, and chanted some spells over them. The next time he went fishing, the leaves had changed into every kind of fish imaginable. Pawang Pukat sold the huge catch and used the money to pay off all his debts.

■

PONGKAPADANG   An ancestor of the Toraja people of Sulawesi. His wife was the water goddess To ri Jenne. He found her stranded on a riverbank after her boat, with her companions still aboard, had floated away while she slept. It is said that parts of the house Pongkapadang first built in Sulawesi can still be seen today.

RANGDA   An evil she-demon in the mythology of the Indonesian people of Bali. Rangda is usually shown naked, with long hair and clawlike fingernails and toenails. She leads a band of witches and is in constant conflict with Barong, the spirit king who represents good.

■

SANGHYANG WIDI WASA   The supreme god of the Indonesian people of Bali. He is also known as Tintiya, meaning "the One who cannot be imagined." All other gods are an aspect of Sanghyang Widi Wasa.

■

SI DEAK PARUJAR   A creator goddess and the daughter of Mula Jadi Na Bolon, the supreme god of the people of Sumatra. In one story, she jumped from Heaven to the Earth to avoid another god. At this time the Earth was only ocean, and she had to float on its waters until her father sent down a little soil, which grew to become the land. The supreme god then sent a hero who battled with NAGA PADOHA, the Underworld serpent, and made the Earth safe. The triumphant hero and Si Deak Parujar produced the first humans to people the new world.

■

SINGA (or SINGA-NAGA)   A fabulous creature in the mythology of the Batak people of northern Sumatra. The Singa is made up of many parts including the horse, the buffalo, the serpent, the dragon, and the elephant. Singa heads are often carved or painted on the sides of houses to protect those inside against evil.

■

TAU TAU   The wooden ancestor figures carved by the Toraja peoples of the Indonesian island of Sulawesi. The figures are portraits of recently deceased people and are clothed and placed high on cliff ledges, so they can be seen from below.

▼ *An elaborate mask of the witch* RANGDA, *worn by Balinese dancers as they reenact the struggle between Rangda and Barong. The Rangda myth may derive from an ancient Balinese queen who was sent away by her husband after she used black magic to destroy half his kingdom.*

· CENTRAL AND · SOUTH AMERICA

Native Americans are thought to have arrived from Asia across a land bridge that existed where the Bering Strait is now. They crossed over in small groups thousands of years ago and spread throughout North America and into South America until they reached the very tip of the continent, probably no later than 7000 B.C.

Many of the people remained hunters, fishers, and food gatherers, but in Central America and Peru, sophisticated cultures grew up. These different levels of development are reflected in the peoples' mythologies. In simple cultures, such as those in the Amazon rain forest, mythological characters are local and behave very much like ordinary people. In contrast, highly organized states, such as those of the Aztecs and the Incas, had a highly structured mythology. Both used mythology to reinforce their power over conquered peoples.

In spite of the differences, common themes are found throughout the region. Sun worship was found in Central American and Andean civilizations. Myths that recall a great flood occur throughout the whole of South America, as does evidence that the jaguar was revered. Human sacrifice was found in many parts of the continent, although probably sacrifice was used to enforce political power even if there was a mythological or religious justification.

▲ The massive ruins of a Mayan pyramid found at Tikal in Guatemala. The city was one of the centers of Mayan civilization.

A Nazca gold mask, which may represent a Sun god. The Nazca civilization was one of the first in South America.

⟶ Route taken by Spanish conquerors
⟶ Spread of Inca people and empire
⟶ Spread of people from North through Mesoamerica

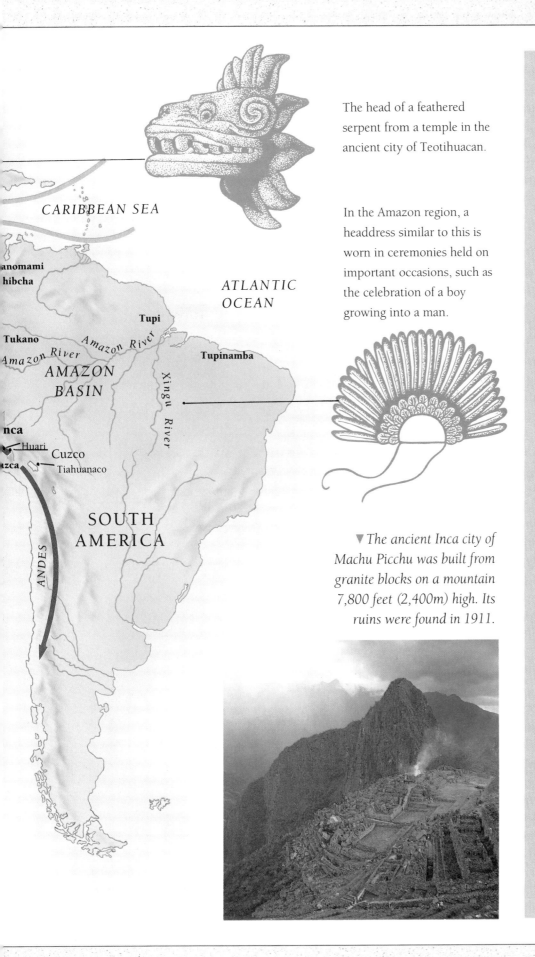

The head of a feathered serpent from a temple in the ancient city of Teotihuacan.

In the Amazon region, a headdress similar to this is worn in ceremonies held on important occasions, such as the celebration of a boy growing into a man.

CARIBBEAN SEA

ATLANTIC OCEAN

anomami
hibcha

Tupi

Tukano

Amazon River

Amazon River

Amazon River

Tupinamba

AMAZON BASIN

Xingu River

nca

Huari

Cuzco

Tiahuanaco

azca

SOUTH AMERICA

ANDES

▼ The ancient Inca city of Machu Picchu was built from granite blocks on a mountain 7,800 feet (2,400m) high. Its ruins were found in 1911.

TIME LINE

B.C.

3372 First date in Mayan calendar

1500 Stone temples are built in Mexico

c. **1200** Olmec civilization develops in Mexico

c. **850** Chavin culture appears in Peru

A.D.

c. **1–650** Nazca civilization flourishes in south Peru

c. **1–750** Mochica civilization flourishes in north Peru

c. **300** In Central America, rise of Mayans and the city of Teotihuacan

c. **950** Toltecs rise to power in Central America

c. **1000** Chimu empire begins to develop in Peru

1151 End of the Toltec empire

c. **1200** The Inca people settle in a valley in the Andes

c. **1325** The Aztecs start to build the city of Tenochtitlan; later on it becomes the center of their empire

c. **1438** The brilliant leader Pachacuti founds the Inca empire

1466 The Incas under Topa defeat the Chimu and take over their lands

1521 The Aztec empire is conquered by the Spanish

1532 The Inca empire is conquered by the Spanish

·MESOAMERICA·

Our knowledge of early beliefs in Mesoamerica (the name used to describe Mexico and Central America before Europeans arrived during the 1500s) comes from the Olmec culture. Arising about 3,000 years ago, the Olmecs may have been the earliest civilization in this part of the world.

The legacy of Olmec mythology appears in later beliefs from Mesoamerica. For example, the Olmecs worshiped a number of different gods, but the jaguar spirit seems to have been especially important. Belief in the jaguar spirit continued in Mesoamerica after the Olmec civilization collapsed. Traces of Olmec gods are found in many later mythologies: early forms of TLALOC, QUETZALCOATL, and TEZCATLIPOCA have possibly been identified in Olmec beliefs.

From Olmec times until the arrival of Europeans, different civilizations rose and faded. The great Mayan culture flourished from around A.D. 250.

Recently, Mayan hieroglyph (picture word) writing has been decoded. This helps us to understand more about Mayan history. Some Mayan books have survived. The best known are the *Popol Vuh* and the *Chilam Balam*, or "Book of the Jaguar."

The Mayans and the Toltecs

The Mayans built many stone cities, developed a calendar, and a system of writing.

Myth and religion played a central part in daily life. Mayans prayed to wind, Earth, plant, rain, and animal gods. Steep pyramids with temples on top were built to honor the gods. Various ceremonies were held throughout the year to honor particular gods.

The Toltec civilization flourished between 900 and 1100, and centered on the capital, Tula. The Toltecs took over myths from peoples who had come before, and at first their chief god was Quetzalcoatl. According to legend, in 987 he was ousted by Tezcatlipoca.

◄ *Four massive stone warriors once held up the roof of the temple at Tula, the Toltec capital. The statues still stand on the roof of the pyramid.*

The Aztecs

By the time the Spanish arrived in 1519, the Aztecs were the dominant culture in Mesoamerica. Many of their beliefs were borrowed from cultures that had come before, such as the Mayans and the Toltecs. The Aztecs also merged the beliefs of conquered peoples into their own collection of gods. This mixture of deities led to a complex mythology that included hundreds of gods, many of whom were not very distinct from one another. Tlaloc, Tezcatlipoca, XIPE TOTEC, and HUITZILOPOCHTLI were all important figures.

◀ An Aztec pendant, showing a double-headed serpent. The pendant probably represents a god and was perhaps worn by a priest during ceremonies to honor the god.

The Aztecs believed that one day Quetzalcoatl would return, signaling the era they lived in had come to an end. In 1519, when the Spanish arrived in Mexico, their leader was thought to be the god returned to take over his kingdom. As a result, the Aztec emperor, Montezuma, let himself be captured. By 1521 the Aztecs were overthrown.

The Aztecs believed that four ages, or "suns," had existed before their own. The first ended when jaguars ate the Earth; the second with a hurricane; the third with fiery rain; and the fourth in a great flood. The fifth sun would end in a great earthquake.

▶ The Mayans played a ball game that had religious importance for them. The aim was to get a ball through hoops, using only hips and elbows. In one story, the twins HUNAHPU and XBALANQUE compete in a ball game against the lords of the Underworld.

▼ *Were-jaguars, or jaguar spirits, were a dominant theme in Olmec mythology. They were half man and half jaguar and usually were shown snarling. These creatures symbolized the supernatural world.*

BACABS Four giant jaguar gods who hold up the sky in Mayan mythology. They stand guard at the four points of the compass, and each has its own color. The east is red, the north is white, the west is black, and the south is yellow.

■

CABRACA An evil giant known as the mountain destroyer in Mayan mythology. Cabraca, the second son of VUCUB-CAQUIX, was destroyed by the hero twins, HUNAHPU AND XBALANQUE. They made him a dish of poisoned wildfowl. When Cabraca ate this, he became so weak that the twins were able to overcome him and bury him alive.

■

CAMAZOTZ A Mayan bat god with very sharp teeth. He attacked the hero twins during their adventure in the Underworld and cut off the head of HUNAHPU. Camazotz is often portrayed with a sacrificial knife in one hand, and his intended victim in the other.

■

CINTEOTL The young Aztec corn god, worshiped as the provider of maize, the most important Aztec crop. Cinteotl is often portrayed wearing a headdress made from maize ears. His name means "maize cob lord," and he is protected by TLALOC.

■

COATLICUE The bloodthirsty Aztec Earth goddess, who wears a skirt of woven snakes. She gave birth to HUITZILOPOCHTLI after a ball of white feathers fell from Heaven and touched her on the breast.

EHECATL The Aztec wind god and an aspect of QUETZALCOATL. He brought physical love to the world when he abducted the beautiful virgin MAYAHUEL from the Underworld. They became lovers by joining together as a glorious tree, with Ehecatl forming one branch and Mayahuel forming the other. Mayahuel's guardian, Tzizimitl, pursued the couple to Earth, and split the tree in two. The branch of Mayahuel was torn to shreds and fed to Tzizimitl's demon servants, but the branch of Ehecatl was left unharmed. Regaining his rightful shape, Ehecatl gathered the bones of Mayahuel and planted them in the fields. From her bones grew a plant that produced white wine.

■

GUCUMATZ A Mayan creator god who took the form of a feathered serpent. He was known as Kukulkan by the Toltecs. Gucumatz and TEPEU created the world, the animals, and the plants. They also created humankind, but only after several unsuccessful tries. First, they made people from mud, but these just crumbled away. Then they tried wood, but these people seemed more like puppets. Next came people made from flesh, but these grew wicked and had to be destroyed. Finally, came people made of maize dough, and these were the Mayan ancestors.

■

HUITZILOPOCHTLI The Aztec war and Sun god who was born fully clothed in blue armor from his mother COATLICUE, with hummingbird feathers decorating his head. He immediately killed his brothers and sisters. The early Aztecs carried his image before them as they searched for their promised land and Huitzilopochtli was said to have been their guide. He became the patron god of the Aztecs, who sacrificed prisoners taken in battle to him.

HUNAHPU AND XBALANQUE The sons of HUN-HUNAHPU, known as the "hero twins" in Mayan mythology. They destroyed the arrogant monster bird VUCUB-CAQUIX and its sons, the giants ZIPACNA and CABRACA. Next, the twins went to the Underworld to avenge their father, who had been killed by the death gods. After a number of ordeals (during which Hunahpu had his head cut off by CAMAZOTZ, but was given a new one by a turtle), the death gods were defeated. The twins then rose to Heaven and became the Sun and the Moon.

HUNHAU The Mayan death god, who is also known as Ah Puch. He has the body of a rotting corpse and is associated with the owl, a symbol of approaching death.

HUN-HUNAHPU A Mayan forefather god. He loved to play ball games, but the noise annoyed the death gods, who tricked him into visiting the Underworld. He was forced to go through a number of trials, and when he failed the death gods cut off his head and hung it on a calabash tree. One day a young girl passed under the tree and the head of Hun-Hunahpu spat into her hand. She became pregnant and gave birth to HUNAHPU AND XBALANQUE.

HURACAN One of the chief Mayan creator gods and the god of storms. The English word "hurricane" comes from his name.

ITZAMNA The supreme Mayan god, who is also known as the "god above all." He taught people the arts of civilization and how to worship the gods.

▶ *The hero twins,* HUNAHPU AND XBALANQUE, *shoot the monster bird* VUCUB-CAQUIX *with their blowpipes.*

▶ *The Aztec death god,* MICHLANTECUHTLI, *ruled over Mictlan. This Underworld was a place of boredom rather than despair.*

MAYAHUEL A beautiful young girl in Aztec mythology who was guarded in the Underworld by an old woman called Tzizimitl. Mayahuel brought physical love to the world when she and EHECATL ran away to Earth and became lovers.

MICHLANTECUHTLI The Aztec god of the dead. With his wife, Mictlantcihuatl, he rules over Mictlan, the dark and gloomy Underworld at the center of the Earth where unworthy spirits go after death.

NANAUTZIN An Aztec god. In a time of darkness the gods decided that they had to sacrifice one of their number to bring light to the world. They were all too afraid, except Nanautzin, who jumped into the flames and reappeared in the east as the Sun.

The Mayan Underworld is called Xibalba. It contains a number of deadly places: the House of Gloom, the House of Cold, the House of Jaguars, and the House of Fire. It was in yet another, the House of Bats, that CAMAZOTZ sliced off HUNAHPU's head.

▼ *A human skull decorated with turquoise stones represents the god* TEZCATLIPOCA. *The eyes of black polished stone symbolize his all-seeing, smoking mirror.*

OMECIHUATL The female aspect of the supreme Aztec deity Ometecuhtli. She gave birth to a stone knife and threw it to Earth, causing 1,600 heroes to rise up. The heroes decided that they needed servants, and with the help of XOLOTL, they created the first man and woman in order to people the Earth with workers.

QUETZALCOATL An important Aztec god who took the form of a feathered serpent. He is a kindly god who unites all the opposing forces in the world. Quetzalcoatl may have developed from a legendary Toltec ruler of the same name. He is said to have given his people maize, science, and the calendar. Sometimes it is not clear whether stories about Quetzalcoatl refer to the god or the king.

In one myth, Quetzalcoatl and his sister slept together after TEZCATLIPOCA made them drunk. On waking, Quetzalcoatl felt so guilty that he built a huge fire and threw himself upon it. The ashes turned into birds that carried his heart to Heaven, where it became the planet Venus, the brightest object in the evening sky.

TECCIZTECATL A proud and noble god in Aztec mythology. When the world was still a dark place, he boasted that he would sacrifice himself in a great fire and return as the Sun. The fire was made, but Tecciztecatl lost his courage and the humble NANAUTZIN jumped into the flames instead. This heroism inspired Tecciztecatl, who followed Nanautzin into the fire and became the Moon.

TEPEU A Mayan creator god who, with GUCUMATZ, created the Earth and all living things. It took many attempts before they were happy with their efforts at making humankind.

TEZCATLIPOCA A Toltec god of pleasure and sin, later adopted as a Sun god by the Aztecs. He is the main enemy of QUETZALCOATL, and causes mischief and confusion in the world. His name means "god of the smoking mirror" and refers to the black mirror he used to replace his foot, which was cut off by the Earth monster in a battle before creation began.

TLALOC The Toltec and Aztec name for the rain god. The Mayans called him Chac. He brings the rain that allows the maize to grow. He wears a net of clouds, a crown of heron feathers, foam sandals, and carries rattles to make thunder. He rules over a paradise called Tlalocan, an Aztec Heaven for those who have drowned.

TONATIUH A Sun god who rules over a paradise called Tollan, an Aztec Heaven for the souls of warriors slain in battle and women who died in childbirth.

VUCUB-CAQUIX In Mayan mythology, a monster in the shape of a bird. It claimed to be a god by pretending to be the Sun and Moon. It was destroyed by the hero twins, HUNAHPU AND XBALANQUE.

XIPE TOTEC The Aztec god of spring and fertility. In an act of self-sacrifice he had his skin removed, symbolizing the young maize shoot breaking out of its husk as it begins to grow. At festivals held in Xipe Totec's honor, priests wore the skins taken from human victims who had been sacrificed as an offering to the god.

XIUHTECUHTLI The Aztec god of fire and time. At the end of every 52 years, the Aztecs renewed time in a special ceremony. All fires were put out and a new fire was lit in the chest of a sacrificed victim.

SACRIFICE

The invading Spaniards were horrified at the number of human sacrifices made by the Aztecs. The slaughter of 20,000 people at a time was not unknown. The victims were usually battle captives. The Aztec Sun god HUITZILOPOCHTLI is said to have told his people, "my mission and my task is war," and his constant need for sacrificial victims reflected the Aztecs' warlike nature. But nearly all the early peoples of Mesoamerica seem to have sacrificed humans, especially at religious festivals. Even children were sacrificed, because their tears were said to encourage the rain. The most common form of Aztec sacrifice was to cut out the victim's heart with a stone knife. The heart was then burned as an offering to Huitzilopochtli.

XOCHIQUETZAL The Aztec goddess of flowers, beauty, and physical love, and patron of silversmiths, sculptors, and painters. Her name means "feather flower." She was married to TLALOC, but the god TEZCATLIPOCA fell in love with her and later abducted her.

XOLOTL An Aztec dog-shaped god, and twin of QUETZALCOATL. In the early days of creation, the first humans were destroyed by the gods. The hero sons of OMECIHUATL lived alone upon the Earth and decided to create new people who would become their servants. They sent Xolotl to the land of the dead to fetch a bone that belonged to one of the first humans. When he returned with the bone, the hero sons sprinkled it with their blood, and from this mixture a boy and girl were born. Xolotl brought the children up on thistle milk, and human life returned to Earth.

YIACATECUHTLI The god of the merchants who crisscrossed Central America right up until the invasion of the Spanish. He was known as the "lord of the nose," because he had a very long nose.

ZIPACNA A giant and the first son of VUCUB-CAQUIX in Mayan mythology. He was so mighty that he could carry mountains on his back. He once tricked 400 warriors into thinking that they had killed him. As they celebrated, he pulled their house down on their heads. They were all killed but reappeared as stars in the night sky.

The gods sent HUNAHPU AND XBALANQUE to destroy Zipacna and his brother, CABRACA. The hero twins tempted Zipacna deep into a mountain cave with a juicy crab, his favorite food. Once he was inside, they pulled the mountain down on top of him.

· THE AMAZON ·

The Amazon basin in South America covers a huge area and crosses many countries. Much of this area is forest, the largest tropical rain forest in the world. People have lived here for thousands of years, depending on the forest and river to support them. As well as hunting and fishing, they have gardens where they grow crops. Most communities live together in large buildings called *malocas*. This is where myths are passed on to other members of the community by the shamans and elders.

In the distant past war was common, and this is reflected in the mythology. Some myths may have begun as the account of a battle that actually took place. As the story was handed down, a myth grew up around the battle.

Most of what we know about myths from the Amazon has been gathered by anthropologists, people who go to live among particular communities, often for long periods. Many of the myths here are from a study carried out in the Xingu region.

Because the societies are small, mythological beliefs are localized, explaining the environment and history of a particular people, as well as their social customs and taboos. Even myths that explain the beginnings of the Sun and Moon have a local setting. The Sun and Moon appear as people from elsewhere, and in the story of MAVUTSINIM, told by people from the Xingu region, they are born after the first man.

◄ *A Kamaiura myth tells how KUAT, the Sun god, brought people daylight. In the beginning everything was dark, people couldn't work, and there was no food. So Kuat kidnapped the bird king, and forced him to give up the day.*

Themes in the myths

Many myths explain how people came to live in a certain area, as in the story of PAHMURI-MAHSE. Myths are often linked to special times in a person's life, such as becoming an adult, marrying, and dying, and so are closely tied to particular ceremonies. Other myths are about customs to do with food.

There are a number of stories about floods, and many myths refer to the river. This shows its importance at the center of life as a source of food and means of transport in the Amazon.

▼ *The story of El Dorado, the gilded man who ruled a city of great riches somewhere in the Amazon region, was a European invention. South American cultures produced fabulous goldwork, such as the pendant shown here, and the myth of El Dorado drove on the Europeans in their greed for gold.*

The peoples of the Amazon believe in a huge number of ogres, demons, and powerful spirits. Many of these spirits take the shape of animals; others are the ghosts of the dead. They can cause either good or bad things to happen and live in a spirit world that exists alongside ours.

Communication with the spirits takes place through the shamans, who are able to enter the spirit world and have a special understanding of it. At times such as ritual ceremonies, the shaman and sometimes the elders will smoke or eat drugs that cause visions. In these they recognize figures from their myths. The shamans then interpret the vision according to the particular occasion. Most peoples have some knowledge of their myths but they are learned and passed on by the shamans and the chiefs.

▼ *It is not only people in the Amazon who have myths about jaguars. Stories about these big cats are found all over Central and South America. They may go back to a very ancient myth about a feline god.*

The peoples of the Amazon have maintained their mythology until quite recently. Myths have been adapted to explain the existence of white people, such as in the story of OMAM, the Yanomami creator god. The native people have opened their mythology to account for the influences of the wider world. However, it is because of these wider influences that the great variety of cultures and vibrant mythologies found in the Amazon are under threat.

▲ ARAVATURA *discovered what happens after death when he followed his best friend's spirit to the battle with the birds.*

A terrifying serpent goddess called Boiuna is said to live in the rivers of the Amazon. She has eyes like lanterns, eats every living thing, and can make women pregnant with just a look.

ARAVATURA   A hero to peoples of the Xingu River region. He discovered the fate of a person's spirit after death, when he went to look for the spirit of a dead friend. He found it with other spirits, all on their way to a battle against the birds. Defeated spirits were eaten by a great eagle. This was the final death. Aravatura returned home ill from the stench of the spirits but was cured by the shamans of his tribe.

AROTEH AND TOVAPOD   Two magicians, according to the Tupi peoples of Brazil. At the start of time men and women lived underground, where there was little to eat. One night some people climbed up through a hole and stole some of the magicians' food. The magicians dug up the hole and hordes of people came out. They were ugly, with webbed feet and boars' tusks, but Aroteh and Tovapod broke off the tusks and reshaped the feet, making them look like the people of today.

IAMURICUMA WOMEN   The people of the Xingu River region tell stories of these warlike women. They turned themselves into spirits and could capture those who looked at them. They are said to have cut off their right breasts in order to draw their bows more easily, just like the Amazons in Greek myth. Such tales were widespread in the Amazon and gave the area its European name.

JURAPARI   In a Tupi myth, the son of a virgin girl. At the time of his birth, women ruled the world, but when Jurapari grew up he took their power away from them and gave it to men. He told the men to hold feasts in celebration of their power. Women were not allowed to attend the feasts, even by accident; if they broke this rule, they were punished with death.

KANASSA   A hero of the Kiukuru people of the Xingu River region. He brought them fire from Heaven and gave the curassow bird its headdress, the alligator its flat tail, and helped ducks to swim.

KUAMUCUCA   A story from the Xingu area tells how Kuamucuca's tribe, with the help of the Sun and Moon, invaded the jaguar village and killed all the jaguars. They collected the claws to make necklaces, but the Sun warned them not to eat the meat. Even now jaguar meat is never eaten.

KUARUP   The name of a festival held by peoples of the Xingu area after someone important has died. MAVUTSINIM, the first man, wanted to bring the dead to life and brought log "kuarups" into the village and dressed them up as people. His plan to bring them to life should have worked — but one man disobeyed Mavutsinim's instructions, and the logs stayed as wood.

KUAT The Kamaiura Sun god. At the beginning of time it was always dark in the world of humans, but light shone in the kingdom of the birds. So Kuat hid himself in a rotting corpse, and when Urubutsin, the king of the birds, arrived to feast on the body, Kuat caught him by the leg. He refused to let go until the bird king agreed to share daylight with people.

MAVUTSINIM The first man, according to one of the peoples of the Xingu River region. One day he was caught by jaguars. In return for his life, he promised them his daughters, but instead he sent wooden substitutes. Two of these girls married jaguars. One became pregnant but was killed by her jealous mother-in-law. Her twin babies survived and grew up to take revenge. These two boys became the Sun and the Moon.

MONAN A Tupinambo creator god who made the Earth, sky, and animals. When the people he had made behaved very badly, Monan destroyed them with a fire. Only one man, Irin-Maje, was saved. Monan put out the fire by sending water, which became the sea. Monan was followed by Maire Monan, who named the different kinds of animals and taught people civilization and agriculture.

OMAM The name of the Yanomami creator god. He takes the shape of a bird. They believe he made everything in the world, from the people in their cities and factories to all the peoples of the Amazon.

▶ *There are many stories about canoes and the river in Amazonian mythology. One example is the tale of* PAHMURI-MAHSE, *who is said to have traveled upriver in a canoe shaped like an anaconda snake.*

PAHMURI-MAHSE A Tukano hero who was ordered by the Sun god to take a huge canoe, shaped like a snake, upriver. Communities were founded everywhere that the canoe stopped. Spirit beings taught the people how to lead their lives.

VALEJDAD According to the Tupi people, Valejdad and his brother Vab were the first men. At the start of the world they were born from a large, beautiful rock, which was a woman. Valejdad was a wicked magician and was eventually exiled in the far north. When he is angry, it rains.

YAJE WOMAN According to the Tukano, a woman who gave birth to a child fathered by the Sun. She rubbed the boy with special shrubs until he was shining and red and then took him to the first men. Each claimed to be the father and tore a piece off the child. In this way each tribe got the special plant that gave them visions of the spiritual world (*see right*).

In many Amazon communities, shamans are trained in the myths of their people and also in traditional medicine. When they wish to enter the spirit world they may eat plants that bring on visions; different tribes use different plants. In their visions, the shamans might see images linked to their myths. The visions help them to advise and heal people.

· SOUTH AMERICA ·

Before the arrival of the Europeans, much of South America was peopled by small communities. But in some places, particularly in the Andes Mountains, a series of highly developed civilizations grew up. These are usually named after their most important cities or archaeological sites. Early civilizations include the Chavin culture, which flourished about 850–200 B.C., the Nazcas (thrived A.D. 1–650), and the Mochicas (flourished A.D. 1–750).

The early gods

Archaeological evidence suggests that early South American mythologies were based on forces of nature. There are many sculptures of beings who are part jaguar, or part serpent, or part condor. Another powerful civilization was based at Tiahuanoco-Huari (A.D. 200–1000). Although almost nothing is known about this culture, it is thought from temple sculptures that people worshiped VIRACOCHA or a similar god.

Reliable evidence about South American mythology is scarce. Unlike in Mesoamerica, the people had no system of writing. Also, as the Incas conquered their neighbors they adapted myths to fit in with their own claims to superiority.

The Chimu people were powerful in Peru from around A.D. 1000 until 1466 when they were defeated by the Incas. Their empire was centered at Chanchan, an enormous walled city. One or two Chimu myths remain. We know that they worshiped a Moon god, called Si, and a sea god, known as Ni. The Chimu claimed that their ancestors had been created by four stars.

◄ *The Incas mummified the bodies of their dead and placed them in stone tombs. The bodies were surrounded by offerings of food, tools, and personal belongings so that each dead person had all he or she needed for life in the next world.*

The Incas

At the time of the Spanish conquest in 1532, the dominant civilization in the Andes was that of the Incas. The Inca empire began to expand about 1438, and by 1525 measured 2,500 miles (4,000 km) from north to south, with the capital, Cuzco, at its center. Religion and myth played an important part in Inca life at every level.

The Incas believed that each age was a reversal of the last, so that what was upper became lower and vice versa. The rule of the Incas was one age, their overthrow by the Spanish was the upheaval, or *pachakuti*, which began the next.

Viracocha was the supreme god and creator. Alongside him, there existed a cult of the Sun, centering on INTI, the Sun god. The Incas claimed that their ancestors were children of the Sun. Their ruler was called the Sapa Inca and, just like his divine ancestors, he usually married his sisters.

Stories about the first Incas were often adapted from older myths that the Incas took over from conquered peoples, such as those about Viracocha and THUNUPA. The gods were said to have brought civilization, teaching irrigation, farming, sewing, and reading.

▶ *The handle of a gold and turquoise ceremonial knife, made by a Chimu craftsman. It was probably made as an offering to a god.*

◀ *The Inca emperor was at the center of the state religion and mythology, claiming INTI as his ancestor. This helped to hold the empire together and strengthened the emperor's rule.*

Outside the Inca empire there were well established mythologies, such as that of the Chibcha people of Colombia. The civilization was conquered by the Spanish in the 1500s.

The Chibcha story of their supreme god, BOCHICA, has much in common with some of the Inca myths about Viracocha and Thunupa. The god was also often identified with the hero NEMTEREQUETEBA. Ancient myths of a supreme creator god are widespread throughout South America.

▶ *The Chibcha god* CHIBCHACUM *supports the world on his shoulders. Whenever he shifts his heavy burden there is an earthquake.*

The first Incas were said to be four brothers and four sisters, known as the Ayar. The brothers were called CUSCO HUANCA, HUANA CUARI, Ayar Manco (MANCO CAPAC), and Topa Ayar Cuchi. The sisters were called CORI OCCLO, Ipa Huaco, Occlo Huaco (MAMA COYA), and Topa Huaco.

Huacas were objects or places that the Incas held sacred. Some were places where something important had happened; others were natural objects such as strangely shaped rocks or mountains. Often these were believed to be the stone forms of spirits or divine beings. Some were irregular rocks regarded as guardians of the fields; others were boundary markers in the fields.

BACHUE   The mother goddess, according to the Chibcha of Colombia, and a protector of crops. Just after the creation of the world, she emerged from a sacred mountain lake with a three-year-old child. When this boy was old enough, Bachue married him and their children were the first people of the world. As soon as their duties as parents were over, Bachue and her husband turned into snakes and returned to the sacred lake.

BOCHICA   The supreme god of the Chibcha, sometimes worshiped as Zue, the Sun god. Bochica is said to have taught humankind the arts of civilization, which explains why he was often linked with the legendary hero, NEMTEREQUETEBA.

CARI AND ZAPANA   Two chieftains in the Collao region of Bolivia, according to Inca legend. Cari asked the Incas for help in his war against Zapana, but the request encouraged the Incas to conquer them both. This legend may be a memory of the fall of Tiahuanoco, an ancient civilization of which almost nothing is known.

CHIBCHACUM   The god of laborers and merchants in Chibcha mythology. He is best known for trying to destroy humankind in a flood. The people were saved by their supreme god, BOCHICA, who struck open the rocks with his golden staff so that the waters could drain away. Then, taking the form of the Sun, he dried the waterlogged land. Chibchacum fled, and since that time he has supported the world on his shoulders.

CONIRAYA   The creator god of the Huarochiri people of Peru. He once came to Earth dressed as a poor man and fell in love with the maiden Cabillaca. He caused a magic fruit to drop near her, and when she ate it Cabillaca became pregnant. She was anxious to know who the father was, so when her son was born she called together all the gods. She told the baby to crawl to his father, and the baby moved toward the ragged Coniraya. Cabillaca was so ashamed that she took her child and jumped into the sea, and they were changed into rocks.

CON TICCI VIRACOCHA   The creator god of the peoples in the Collao region of Peru, who predates VIRACOCHA, the supreme Inca god. He is said to have created the Sun and to have made stone models of every tribe of people, which he placed throughout the land. Then he traveled across the region bringing the stone images to life and ordering them to worship him.

CORI OCCLO   One of the first Inca sisters. According to one myth, she was sent ahead to find somewhere to settle and chose the city of Cuzco, which took its name from the second Inca brother, CUSCO HUANCA.

CUSCO HUANCA
The second of the first Inca brothers. In one of the myths that explain the origin of the Incas, he is said to have been the first ruler of Cuzco. (*See also* MANCO CAPAC.)

EKKEKO A household god of the highland people of Peru. He is shown as a small man with a round belly and is covered with toy household utensils. According to one story, he is the ruler of a miniature city. Miniature images of Ekkeko were seen as good luck charms, and they are still bought today in the hope that they will bring marriage and good fortune.

HUANA CAURI The eldest of the first Inca brothers. He did not go to Cuzco with his brothers and sisters but chose to stop at a mountain, which was renamed Huana Cauri in his memory. In another story, he is known as Ayar Cachi, who showed off all the time. In the end, this annoyed his family so much that they walled him up inside the mountain.

HUATHIACURI
The son of PARIACACA, the storm god of the people of west Peru. He once met a rich man whose wife had committed adultery. Her sin caused two serpents to eat away her husband's life. The serpents died when Huathiacuri made the wife confess, and the man was saved.

HUITACA An evil Chibcha goddess. As patron of drunkenness and misbehavior, she came to Earth and tried to undo the good works of NEMTEREQUETEBA, who had taught humankind the civilized arts. She is sometimes known as Chia, the Moon goddess and wife of the Sun god Zue (*see* BOCHICA). One story says that Huitaca was turned into the Moon by Nemterequeteba.

IMAYMANA VIRACOCHA The son of the Inca creator god, VIRACOCHA. He traveled to the mountains and valleys giving names to all the plants and instructed the people which were good to eat and which were useful for medicine. His younger brother, Tocapo Viracocha, did the same in the lowlands.

▼ *There are various legends that explain the origin of the Incas. In one, all Incas are said to descend from the Sun god* INTI, *who sent his children* MANCO CAPAC *and* MAMA COYA *to Earth to bring civilized ways to the people.*

In another legend, the first Incas were four brothers and four sisters known as the Ayar. They emerged from a cave at Paccari-Tambo, which was near the site of the city of Cuzco. One brother, Manco Capac, married one of the sisters, Occlo Huaco (Mama Coya), and they became the first Inca king and queen. From that time, it was traditional for the Inca ruler to marry his sister, who then took the title Coya.

▼As an emperor enters Cuzco, the Inca capital, he is welcomed by the Virgins of the Sun, who had received up to seven years' training in religious duties. Between them sits the mummified body of a former emperor. A gold mask, representing the Sun god INTI, *is on the wall behind the mummy.*

INTI   The Sun god of the Incas. He is their most senior god after VIRACOCHA, and probably the most important god in everyday worship. The Incas believed that they were descended from Inti, who sent his children MANCO CAPAC and MAMA COYA to Earth to rule and civilize the savage people living there. Because Viracocha is so remote, Inti is often wrongly thought to be the supreme god of the Incas.

KHUNO   A snow and storm god of the people in the high valleys of the Andes. When the people began burning the forests to clear the land for farming, the smoke blackened the snow on the mountaintops. Khuno was so angry that he sent a great flood, and the people only survived by hiding in caves. When the waters went down, the people went looking for food. They found a new shrub, the coca plant, and as they chewed its leaves they lost all sense of hunger, cold, and unhappiness.

MAMA COYA   In one story, she is the daughter of INTI, the Inca Sun god. In another, she is known as Occlo Huaco, one of the first Inca sisters. Both stories agree that she married her brother MANCO CAPAC and became the first Inca queen.

MANCO CAPAC   The first Inca ruler. One story says that he is the son of the Sun god INTI. A less heroic version says that he was just a man who dressed in silver and went to the top of a mountain where he let the Sun shine on him. His dazzling appearance so impressed the local people that they accepted him as the son of the Sun.

NEMTEREQUETEBA   A legendary hero of the Chibcha of Colombia. He was a preacher who traveled the country teaching both civilized behavior and the art of weaving. Nemterequeteba was said to be an old man with long hair and a long beard, from a distant land.   (*See also* BOCHICA, THUNUPA.)

PACHACAMAC A creator god of the coastal peoples of Peru, and child of the Sun and Moon. An earlier god called Con created the first people, but Pachacamac overthrew him and turned these people into monkeys. He then created a new couple but did not give them any food, and the man died. The woman gave birth to a child, who taught her how to live off wild plants. This angered Pachacamac, who killed the child, but maize and other crops grew from the dead body. Pachacamac was later identified with the Inca supreme god, VIRACOCHA.

PACHAMAMA The Earth mother of the Incas, and goddess of all plants and animals. Later, Christians identified her with Mary, the mother of Jesus Christ.

PARIACACA The god of storm and flood, worshiped by the people of west Peru. He defeated his rival, the fire god, who fled to the mountains. Pariacaca chased him, but the fire god escaped into the rain forest, leaving behind an enormous two-headed serpent, which Pariacaca turned into stone.

THUNUPA A legendary preacher hero of the Incas whose story is similar to that of VIRACOCHA and NEMTEREQUETEBA. He is described as a middle-aged white man with a beard and gray hair, who traveled the land performing miracles and preaching to the people about moral behavior. Some Europeans believed that he may have been Thomas, one of the Twelve Apostles, the first followers of Jesus Christ. Many stories about him seem to have been influenced by Christianity. (*See also* BOCHICA.)

TUTUJANAWIN A supreme god of the people of Peru, who was described as "the beginning and the end of all things." He is said to be the power which gave life and energy to everything in the universe.

VIRACOCHA The supreme god of the Incas and the creator of all things. He is said to be invisible and ever-present, but is often portrayed as an old man with a long beard. After creating humankind, Viracocha taught them the arts of civilization, and he has much in common with the preacher heroes NEMTEREQUETEBA and THUNUPA, with whom he is sometimes confused. Viracocha is an ancient god, and was worshiped in many forms by several pre-Inca cultures, before being adopted by the Incas themselves. He became a very remote god and ruled through more active gods such as INTI.

YLLAPA The Inca thunder god, who is usually portrayed holding a war club in one hand and a sling in the other.

▲ *The thunder god* YLLAPA *collects water from the Milky Way and stores it in a jug. The water is released as rain when Yllapa shatters the jug with a stone from his sling. Thunder is said to be the crack of the sling, and a lightning bolt the stone sent flying toward its mark.*

The Incas worshiped the planet Venus as the goddess Chasca, who watched over flowers and young girls. Other planets were seen as the handmaidens of the Moon.

· SOUTH PACIFIC · LANDS

Scattered across a huge area in the Pacific Ocean are thousands of islands, known by the group name of Oceania. These islands can be divided into three main groups: Melanesia, Micronesia, and Polynesia.

The first people arrived in the Pacific islands thousands of years ago, traveling in small groups from Southeast Asia, and settled in Melanesia and Micronesia. Most of the islands of Polynesia were settled later; people only reached New Zealand around A.D. 750. The societies remained fairly unchanged until the arrival of Europeans, who introduced Christianity in the 1800s.

Australia, which is also in the South Pacific, is a continent, and so is not counted as part of Oceania. Its native population is the Aborigines, who have lived there at least 50,000 years.

There is a great variety among the peoples of Oceania and Australia, both physically and in their cultures and mythologies. Echoes of Indian and Asian myths are found, but most Oceanic mythology explains the natural world, how different communities began, and how they got their laws and customs. Many myths reflect the seafaring way of life and the importance of the Pacific Ocean. Ancestor heroes are also important.

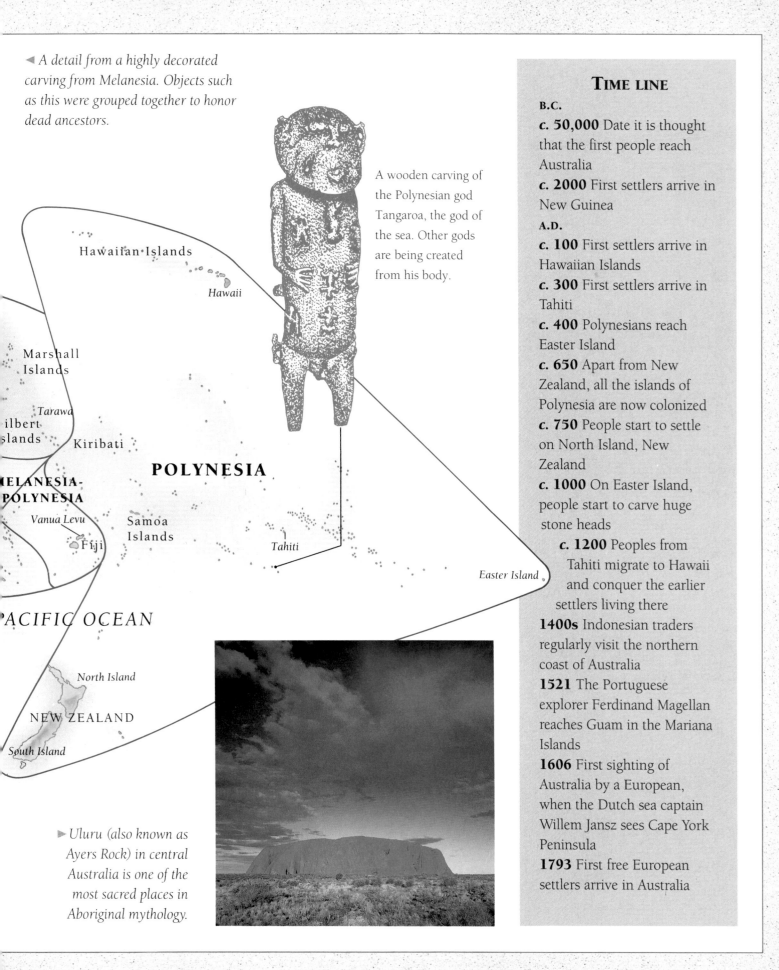

◄ *A detail from a highly decorated carving from Melanesia. Objects such as this were grouped together to honor dead ancestors.*

A wooden carving of the Polynesian god Tangaroa, the god of the sea. Other gods are being created from his body.

Hawaiian Islands

Hawaii

Marshall Islands

Tarawa

ilbert
slands

Kiribati

POLYNESIA

MELANESIA-
POLYNESIA

Vanua Levu

Samoa Islands

Fiji

Tahiti

Easter Island

PACIFIC OCEAN

North Island

NEW ZEALAND

South Island

► *Uluru (also known as Ayers Rock) in central Australia is one of the most sacred places in Aboriginal mythology.*

· SOUTH PACIFIC ·
LANDS

Since the late 1800s, most people in Oceania have been Christians. Before this time, people revered a number of different gods, goddesses, or spirits, and rich mythologies flourished on the different islands.

Melanesia

Melanesia stretches from New Guinea, the largest island in Oceania, east to Fiji. The greatest number of languages are spoken in this region: there are more than 700 in New Guinea alone. Many of the communities live in small groups in mountain valleys, often isolated from each other. Not surprisingly, there is a wide range of mythology, but there are some common themes.

The idea of "mana" is important throughout Melanesia. Mana is a supernatural power that is present everywhere. It is possible for a person to channel the power, but this is always at the risk that it may burst out in a new form.

Melanesian myths do not often explain the beginning of time, or how the universe was created. Instead, it is assumed to have always existed. Myths that explain where human beings came from are more common. For example, in a myth that features the sky-being KAMBEL, the first people come out of a tree. Many communities have myths about animals, such as snakes or crocodiles, which they say are their ancestors. Snakes can be particularly powerful: as far apart as New Guinea and Fiji, stories are told about snake or serpent gods responsible for great floods.

◄ *Some Melanesian myths explain how the sea was released, separating island from island, and inland peoples from seagoing peoples. Myths relating to the sea, or the seafaring way of life, are widespread throughout Oceania.*

As a boy, OLOFAT went to search for his father in the sky realm. He came across some workmen building a house for the spirits of the dead. Because the boy was a stranger, the men tried to crush him in the foundations of the building. Olofat escaped (with the help of some termites) and climbed to the rafters of the house, shouting and terrifying everyone.

Myths about heroes and tricksters are also popular, such as the stories about QAT and TAKARO. Sometimes the myths feature two or more brothers, who are often at war with each other. For example, the hero To Kabinaba is a great help to humanity, while his twin To Karvuvu causes nothing but trouble. It is his fault that death came to the world. At first, people were able to shed their skins to stay young, but when To Karvuvu's mother shed her skin he did not recognize her and became upset. She put her old skin back on, and since then people grow old and die.

Micronesia

Micronesia (which includes Kiribati and the Marshall, Caroline, and Mariana islands) has the smallest population in Oceania. Micronesian myths are often similar to those found in Polynesia, although the characters have different names. For example, the story of land being pulled up from the sea is popular in both areas. In one Micronesian creation myth, the Earth and the sky were close together—until the spider creator NAREAU had them pushed apart. This myth is similar to the Polynesian story of PAPA AND RANGI.

Many Micronesian myths reflect the seafaring way of life, as in the stories about Alulei, the god of navigation. He was killed by his jealous brothers but brought back to life by his father, who gave him thousands of eyes as protection. These are now said to be the stars that guide sailors.

There is some evidence of belief in supreme gods, but there is greater interest in the more human hero and trickster descendants such as Nareau, Motitik, and OLOFAT. Ancestor worship is traditionally important. On the Gilbert Islands people regularly made offerings both to the gods and to their divine ancestors.

Many societies in Micronesia had a rich oral literature and their poets or storytellers were highly thought of. But, as elsewhere, much of this culture was destroyed by the arrival of the Europeans.

According to the Gilbert Islanders, the first ancestor was Taburimai. His parents were fish gods and his brother a shark spirit, but Taburimai himself had a human shape and married a mortal woman. His son wed a tree goddess.

In Polynesian mythology, certain objects or words are "taboo"—they must not be touched or mentioned. This is because they are linked to something holy and powerful, or else to something unclean. People, such as the chief or priest, may also be taboo.

Polynesia

Polynesia stretches in a huge triangle from New Zealand to Hawaii to Easter Island. Despite the vast distances between these islands, similar stories are found throughout the area—although sometimes names may be slightly different, or different parts of a story are given more importance.

These similarities occur because as Polynesians settled new islands, they took their mythology with them. The journeys to these new lands are remembered and celebrated in the legends of heroes, who undertook great voyages to faraway places such as the Sun, the Moon, and the Underworld.

Like many Polynesian societies, Polynesian mythology is more organized than that of other places in Oceania. For instance, there is a "family tree" of Polynesian gods made up of Papa, Rangi, and their children.

In New Zealand and elsewhere, schools, called "whares" by the Maoris, taught mythology and religion. Priests and chiefs were responsible for passing on myths and conducting rituals and ceremonies. In some regions, entertainers traveled from place to place, acting out myths.

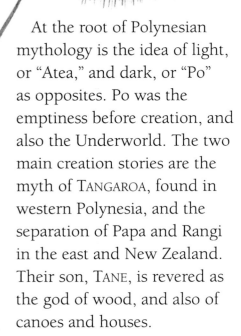

At the root of Polynesian mythology is the idea of light, or "Atea," and dark, or "Po" as opposites. Po was the emptiness before creation, and also the Underworld. The two main creation stories are the myth of TANGAROA, found in western Polynesia, and the separation of Papa and Rangi in the east and New Zealand. Their son, TANE, is revered as the god of wood, and also of canoes and houses.

Another important figure is the goddess HINE, who rules the Underworld. But perhaps the best known figure in Polynesian myth is the trickster hero MAUI, who struggles with the gods on behalf of humanity.

◄ *The hero* MAUI *once caught the Sun in a noose and beat it so that it could only creep along the sky. This made the days longer.*

Aboriginal myths

For thousands of years the Aborigines of Australia were wanderers, hunting for their food. In 1788, when settlers from Europe first reached Australia, there were about 300,000 Aborigines living there. They were badly treated by the Europeans, who saw them as primitive peoples and did not understand them. The new settlers did not appreciate that although the Aborigines had few possessions, they had a rich, complex mythology.

Aboriginal religion and myth are closely linked to the land and the natural world. The landscape is said to have been shaped by the ancestor spirits during the Dreamtime, an era before living memory.

These spirits took both human and animal shape, and gave parts of themselves to form the landscape, such as their tails for trees. They also made people and the various animals and plants, and laid down the laws and customs by which people were to live. Once the work was done, the spirits went back to sleep.

▶ *Aborigines hold ceremonies to renew the links with their ancestors. During these they paint themselves with certain markings, dance, and sing.*

People today are linked to these ancestors through totem groups. Totems are often animals. Each is tied to a particular spirit center established in the Dreamtime.

A woman is said to become pregnant when a spirit child enters her. The totem of the newborn child depends on where the mother was at the time. A person learns about his or her totemic history of "dreaming" during initiation rites and in turn becomes responsible for passing it on.

Although the Dreamtime is in the distant past, it becomes part of the present when myths are acted out in ritual. People taking part in these rituals briefly become the ancestor, as they trace their journey again.

The boomerang was an important weapon to the Aborigines, who used it to kill animals they were hunting. According to a myth told by the Binbinga of northern Australia, it was invented by the snake Bobbi-bobbi, who made it from one of his ribs.

Aborigines pass on their myths orally, and through rock, sand, and bark paintings. In the north, cave paintings of the Dreamtime spirit are retouched every year, just before the wet season. This renews the protection offered by the spirit.

HINE is also known as the goddess of the Moon, having traveled there by canoe. When there is a full Moon, Hine can be seen beating the bark of a tree to make cloth.

▼ KAMBEL *heard noises from the trunk of a tree and found the first people inside it.*

BAIAME   A creator god and sky hero in Australian mythology. Baiame is known by different names, including Daramulun, Ngurunderi, and Bunjil. He is thought to have made all the features of the landscape, such as the rivers, hills, and trees.

■

BUE   A hero of the Gilbert Islanders in Micronesian mythology. He was the son of the Sun god and a mortal woman. Bue demanded that his father teach him wisdom. The Sun taught him crafts, rituals, and knowledge of the weather. The hero passed this on to his people.

■

DJANGGAWUL   Australian sky spirits, two sisters and a brother who traveled the Earth. The Djanggawul sisters were constantly having children whose father was also their brother. In this way they peopled the land. They also created water holes, plants, and trees, and gave the people their sacred emblems and rituals.

■

HINE   TANE's wife in Polynesian mythology. One day, to her horror, she discovered that she was also his daughter and fled in shame to the Underworld. This is how Hine-titama, the dawn maiden, became the terrible Hine-nui-te-Po, the goddess of darkness and death.

▲ *A scene from an aboriginal bark painting, showing the* DJANGGAWUL *sisters giving birth to the first people.*

IO   In Maori mythology, an all-powerful god. It is now thought that his importance may be only a recent development, and beliefs about him have probably been influenced by Christianity.

■

IWA   A trickster in Hawaiian mythology. It is said he owned a magic paddle that took him from one end of Hawaii to the other in only four strokes.

■

KAMBEL   A Papuan sky god. He heard sounds coming from a tree trunk. Inside were the first people. Kambel caused the tree to open up and release them into the world. Later, the god saw a shining object rise from the tree. He tried to reach it, but it slipped away and became the Moon.

KUNAPIPI A mother goddess who is important in Arnhem Land in northern Australia. She formed the land from her body and made children, animals, and plants. She is also goddess of death and rebirth who swallows people, usually children or young men, but then vomits them up again so that they are released.

■

LIGOUBUBFANU A Micronesian creator goddess and the wife of the sky god, Anulap. According to the Truk Islanders, Ligoububfanu made their island as well as people, plants, and animals.

■

MAKE-MAKE The creator god of Easter Island in Polynesia, who made humankind. He was also patron of the bird cult. Each year the first person to find a bird's egg became the Bird Man for one year. His hair, eyebrows, and eyelashes were shaved and he was carried down the mountain to a place where he lived by himself for the rest of the year.

■

MAUI The best known Polynesian hero and trickster who did many things to help humankind. He fished up the islands of Polynesia from the bottom of the sea, using a magic hook. He also caught the Sun in a noose to slow it down as it raced across the sky. This was to give people more time in the day to cook their meals.

Maui died while trying to win eternal life for humans from HINE-nui-te-Po. The hero and his friends, the birds, went to the Underworld, where they found the goddess asleep. Warning the birds not to laugh, he crept into her body intending to come out through her mouth. But it was such a funny sight that one bird did laugh. Hine-nui-te-Po woke up and squeezed her insides together, crushing Maui. As a result, humans cannot escape from death.

NAKAA According to the Gilbert Islanders in Micronesia, Nakaa was the first judge. He lived in the paradise of Matang. Men and women lived separately there, and each sex had its own tree. But when Nakaa went away, the men disobeyed his instructions and joined the women. After this, their hair began to turn gray. When he came back and found what had occurred, Nakaa banished the people but allowed them to take one tree with them. They chose the women's tree, which was death. Nakaa tore leaves from the tree and threw them at the people. From then on disease and death came into the world.

■

NAREAU In Micronesian mythology, a supreme god, or in some accounts, two gods, father and son, in the shape of spiders. The name means "Sir Spider." Nareau supervised creation, including the separation of Heaven and Earth by Riiki, the eel. In other stories, Nareau is a trickster figure who is said to have created the islands of Tarawa, Beru, and Tabutenea by throwing blossoms into the sea.

▲ *Each year the people of Easter Island carried the Bird Man down the mountain to a place where he would live as a hermit for the next 12 months. (See* MAKE-MAKE.*)*

The "Cargo Cult" is a modern belief that first appeared in Papua New Guinea in 1920 and still exists in parts of Melanesia. Its members believe that the gods wish them to have a share of the wealth Westerners enjoy. They believe that a ship will arrive one day, crewed by the spirits of their ancestors, and it will bring wonderful gifts.

OLOFAT A Micronesian trickster, son of a mortal woman and the sky god, Luk. He is a mischievous character who eventually took on the role as go-between from his father to human beings, passing on his father's wishes—although he sometimes caused trouble when he added his own twists to these commands. In a more helpful spirit, he sent people the gift of fire, held in the beak of a bird.

PAPA AND RANGI In the creation myth of New Zealand and eastern Polynesia, Papa was the Earth Mother, and Rangi the Sky Father. Rangi clasped Papa in what seemed to be an endless embrace. He held her so tightly that Papa's children were trapped inside her. These were the unborn gods, who decided that they had to force their parents apart in order to escape. Papa and Rangi were separated by their son TANE, the god of forests, who simply lifted the Sky Father with his head and pushed the Earth Mother down with his feet.

PELE The Hawaiian volcano goddess who lives in the crater of Kilauea on Hawaii. One myth tells how Pele sent her young sister Hi'iaka to fetch her lover, Lohiau, from his home. But as she waited for their arrival, Pele became suspicious of the pair and ultimately tried to kill them. Lohiau died, but Hi'iaka survived and found his spirit which she reunited with his body, bringing him back to life.

▲ *At first,* PAPA AND RANGI *were locked together in so close an embrace that their children, the gods, were trapped between them. Eventually, their son* TANE *managed to push them apart.*

QAT A Melanesian trickster. Some of his adventures are similar to those of MAUI. Qat was born from a stone on the island of Vanua Levu. His constant companion is Marawa, a spider. While Qat brought life into the world, Marawa introduced death. The two are associated with canoe-building and seafaring.

▶ *According to one story,* PELE *was deserted by her husband. She cried so much that Hawaii was flooded with her tears, and only the highest peaks could be seen.*

RANGI *see* **PAPA and RANGI**

TAKARO A Melanesian hero who is similar in many ways to QAT. Takaro once saw a sky maiden bathing, so he stole her wings and made her his wife. He put her to work in his yam patch, where ripe yams fell into her hands. Takaro's brothers refused to believe the fruits were ripe and scolded her. She stood in her doorway crying until her tears uncovered her hidden wings. She flew back to the sky, taking her child with her. Takaro tried to follow her by climbing up a banyan vine, but she cut it so that he fell to his death.

TANE A Polynesian god of forests, and patron of canoe-making and all work with wood. He is the son of PAPA AND RANGI, and separated the Earth from the sky. It was Tane who decorated the heavens with stars and set the Sun and Moon in their places. Later, Tane wanted a wife, so he made a woman out of clay and breathed life into her. He called the woman Hine and married her. Their children were the first Polynesian people. Tane married one of his daughters. She was also called HINE.

TANGAROA   The sea god in Polynesian mythology. In the beginning, only the ocean existed, and Tangaroa sent a bird called Tuli over the waters. It could find nowhere to rest so Tangaroa threw down a rock, and this became one of the Manu'a islands. Then Tuli complained that the island was too exposed to the Sun, so Tangaroa gave the bird a creeping vine for shade. This was known as the "Peopling Vine" because when it eventually withered and decayed, maggots were formed, and these developed into the first people.

TAWHAKI   A great Polynesian hero and the grandfather of another hero, Rata. Although some say his mother was a goddess, he is valued more as a human being of great courage and nobility.

TAWHIRI   The Polynesian god of winds and storms, and the son of PAPA AND RANGI. He did not want his parents to be forced apart and sent winds to attack TANE's forests and the seas of TANGAROA (according to this myth, god of the ocean). Some of Tangaroa's reptiles fled to the forest so Tangaroa and Tane (ocean and land) have been enemies ever since.

TU   The Polynesian war god and son of PAPA AND RANGI. In Hawaii, he is known as Ku. Tu fought TAWHIRI and then turned on his other brothers because they did not help him. This was seen as the beginning of warfare.

WALWALAG SISTERS   Australian sky beings. While traveling with their babies, they offended the Great Rainbow Snake, YURLUNGGUR, by accidentally polluting the waterhole in which the creature lived. The sisters sang and danced to try and keep him at bay, but he swallowed them and their children.

Later, the snake vomited the sisters up, and green ants bit them and restored them to life. Their story is reenacted in a song-drama of the people of Arnhem Land.

YABWAHINE   A Melanesian sky god who taught people which animals to hunt and how to look after their gardens.

YURLUNGGUR   One of the many names for the Australian Great Rainbow Snake. It is not always clear whether the snake is male or female. In Arnhem Land it can be one form of the goddess KUNAPIPI. The snake, like other sky beings, was a creator of the landscape, particularly rivers and water holes. It is closely associated with a concern for fertility, both in humans and in nature.

▼ *A rock painting of the Great Rainbow Snake, an ancestor who helped to make rivers in the dry land. In some myths, the snake caused a great flood that washed away the world that existed before this one.*

The serpent's body stretches across the sky as the rainbow. It has many different names, including YURLUNGGUR, and is one of the most important ancestor spirits in Aboriginal mythology.

GLOSSARY

A list of definitions for significant or unusual words found in this book

AVATAR   The human or animal form taken by a Hindu DEITY, who has descended from Heaven to Earth.

CHAOS   The state of the universe before creation, often thought of as a watery, shapeless space.

CHARM   A spell or object, thought to possess SUPERNATURAL power, which brings good luck.

CULT   A set of religious beliefs, where the main object of worship is often a person, or an unusual idea.

DEITY   A SACRED being, especially a god or goddess.

DEMIGOD   A half-god; a child who has a god or goddess and a human as parents.

DEMON   An evil SPIRIT, which tries to defeat or destroy good.

DIVINATION   The practice of trying to learn about future events, or get messages from the gods, through SUPERNATURAL means.

FOLKLORE   Any of the ancient and traditional customs, beliefs, or stories of a people.

HEAVEN   The home of gods, goddesses and sometimes the SOULS of people who have led perfect lives. It is often thought to be a beautiful world above the Earth.

IMMORTAL   A living creature that will never die or cannot be killed.

KAMI   A type of DEITY in the Shinto religion of Japan. It inhabits every feature of the landscape and all the natural elements.

LEGEND   A story that has grown up around a heroic figure, who may once have been a real person. Such stories may have been handed down by word of mouth from generation to generation.

MANA   A SUPERNATURAL power that inhabits any special or extraordinary object or person, in traditional Melanesian belief.

MEDICINE MAN   A SHAMAN in Africa and North America, who acts as a healer, diviner, and moral leader.

ORACLE   A place where priests or priestesses reveal the will of the gods or foretell the future. The word also describes the priest or priestess.

ORAL TRADITION   The passing on of the myths, history, and customs of a people from generation to generation by word of mouth.

PROPHECY   A statement about future or unknown events, which is inspired by the gods; or a message from the gods.

REINCARNATION   The rebirth of a dead person's SOUL in a new body.

RITUAL   A set of formal, symbolic actions, which form part of religious worship. An important event in someone's life, such as birth, coming of age, marriage, or death, may also be marked by a ritual.

SACRED   The most essential parts of any religion; anything that is holy.

SACRIFICE   The RITUAL offering of gifts to a DEITY, as thanks for a past favor, or in hope of future help. The gift can be an animal or human victim, but more often is symbolic.

SHAMAN   A healer, prophet, diviner, or MEDICINE MAN whose SUPERNATURAL powers are said to arise from contact with the SPIRIT world.

SHRINE   A place which has become SACRED because it is closely connected with a person or an event that is important to a religion.

SOUL   The part of a being which thinks and feels. The soul is said to be IMMORTAL, and on the death of the body it goes to HEAVEN or the UNDERWORLD, or is reborn in another body.

SPIRIT   A living being that has no body. It influences events in the world for good or bad. The word can also mean the SOUL, or the life-giving energy the soul carries.

SUPERNATURAL   Something which exists outside the laws of nature; magical or spiritual.

TABOO   A ban imposed on objects or actions for SACRED reasons.

TOTEM   A SACRED object or animal, respected by a group of people as a symbol and protector of the group.

UNDERWORLD   The home of SOULS, usually thought to be a land below the Earth. It is sometimes seen as a place of horror and misery, and sometimes as a place of judgment where the fate of souls is decided.

INDEX

Page numbers in **bold** indicate sections or glossary entries; page numbers in *italics* show illustrations; words in SMALL CAPITALS indicate geographical chapters; words in **bold** indicate sub-sections

The publishers wish to thank the following artists
for their contribution to this book:

Hemesh Alles (Maggie Mundy) 94, 102–103, 104–105, 106–107, 108;
Karin Ambrose 134t; David Anstey 16, 32t, 55t, 58b, 66tl, 72t,
78t, 102t, 116t, 122tl, 138t; Marion Appleton 109; Noel Bateman 51b;
Richard Berridge (SPECS) 46–47, 48–49, 96t, 97, 124–125, 134–135b,
136–137; Maggie Brand (Maggie Mundy) 82; Vanessa Card all borders, 73t, 74b;
Peter Dennis (Linda Rogers Assoc.) 28–29, 30–31, 36–37, 38–39,
40–41, 44–45, 50, 51t, 52, 53b, 98–99; Alan Fraser (Pennant) 18–19, 75, 76–77;
Eugene Fleury all maps; Terry Gabbey 70; Donald Harley (B. L. Kearley Ltd.)
78–79, 84–84, 86–87, 88–89, 90–91, 92–93, 95; Adam Hook (Linden Artists) 23,
33b, 34, 66–67, 67, 122tr, 123, 139b, 145–147, 148–149, 150–151, 152–153;
John James (Temple Rogers) 27; Roger Jones (SPECS) 35, 68–69: 128b, 129b,
130–131, 132–133, 138b, 140–141, 142–143;
Kevin Maddison 53t; Angus McBride (Linden Artists) 113b, 72–73b, 74;
Nicki Palin 116tr, 117b, 118, 120–121; Mark Peppé 16–17;
Bernard Robinson 21, 22, 24–25; 26, 26–27, 70–71; Tony Smith (Virgil Pomfret) 83b;
Andrew Wheatcroft (Virgil Pomfret) 56–57, 58t, 59, 60–61, 62–63;
Paul Young (Artist Partners) 110–111, 112–113, 114–115

The publishers wish to thank the
following for supplying photographs for this book:

14 Zefa; 15 Comstock; 16 WFA; 22 WFA;
33 Larousse plc/National Museum, Copenhagen;
42 WFA/Statens Historiska Museum; 43 WFA; 45 WFA;
54 Andoni Canela/TRIP; 55 ZEFA; 57 WFA;
64 Cracknell/TRIP; 65 ZEFA; 73 WFA/Private collection; 100 ZEFA
101 ZEFA; 119 Michael Holford; 125 WFA/Denpasar Museum, Bali;
126 ZEFA; 127 ZEFA; 144 C. M. Dixon; 145 ZEFA; 152 Michael Holford

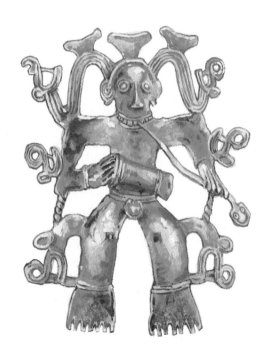